give my head peace

The Hole in the Wall Gang, 1999

give my head peace

THE BOOK

The Hole in the Wall Gang

THE
BLACKSTAFF PRESS

BELFAST

acknowledgements

Thanks to everyone for making *Give My Head Peace* such a success, in particular our director Martin Shardlow, Stephen Butcher (director of *Two Ceasefires and a Wedding*), our producer Jackie Hamilton, our script editor Niall Leonard (for axing all our weaker gags and suggesting funny alternatives) and all the actors and crew who have worked on the series. All photographs courtesy of the BBC press office. Thanks to the BBC for letting us get away with it and especially executive producer Paul Evans for letting us say 'fuck' for the first time ever on a local television programme.

First published in 1999 by
The Blackstaff Press Limited
Blackstaff House, Wildflower Way, Apollo Road
Belfast BT12 6TA, Northern Ireland

The Hole in the Wall Gang Limited has asserted its right under the Copyright, Designs and Patents Act 1988 to be identified as the author of this work.

Designed by Dunbar Design

Printed in Ireland by ColourBooks Limited

A CIP catalogue record for this book
is available from the British Library

ISBN 0-85640-669-4

Contents

The scriptwriters (from left): Damon Quinn, Michael McDowell and Tim McGarry

give my head peace
an introduction

Give My Head Peace went through a more convoluted and tortuous development than the peace process. It was inspired as a satirical counterblast to two particularly pernicious types of Northern Ireland play that seemed to predominate stage and screen in the 1970s and 1980s. The first type was what Stephen Rea has called 'balaclava' plays – the kind of *Harry's Game* nonsense where all terrorists are psychopathic twitchers played by English actors with dodgy Northern Ireland accents. The other type was what we call 'why can't it all be like Corrymeela' plays, which usually featured star-crossed lovers thwarted by the sectarian divide. Both of these types of play invariably end with, as Uncle Andy says in *Two Ceasefires and a Wedding*, 'the inevitable tragic denouement'.

The origins of *Give My Head Peace* can be traced back to 1987 and a sketch performed for a Queen's University Third World Society charity review. Set in Divis Flats, it featured a dialogue between two characters that effectively became Ma and Emer.

MA
Look at all the condescension

EMER
By the author?

MA
No, I mean look at all the damp.

EMER
Ma, how come you always mispronounce your words?

MA
I don't know, Graham Reid said something about comedy elements.

EMER
You mean it's the only way of saving the credibility of this shite awful play.

MA
Emer! I taught you never to swear, I sent you to electrocution lessons and all.

Needless to say, the sketch ends with Ma being informed that her son has been kneecapped for joyriding and another daughter has been tarred and feathered for going out with a Prod. Another sketch from the same period, *Too Late to Talk to Billy and Paddy About Love Across the Barricades in the Terror Triangle*, lampooned the genre from a homosexual angle.

We decided after leaving university that we didn't want to be lawyers and could have a much more worthwhile career writing and performing silly sketches for radio. It was in the BBC Radio Ulster series *A Perforated Ulster* that a weekly radio soap featuring all the characters we now know in *Give My Head Peace* appeared for the first time. This was then turned into a half-hour radio play for BBC Radio 4 and finally BBC Northern Ireland agreed to produce and broadcast a programme for local television. *Two Ceasefires and a Wedding* proved to be a spectacular success, earning great ratings and winning a Royal Television Society Award.

We had intended *Two Ceasefires and a Wedding* to be a one-off but a chat in a bar with playwright Martin Lynch and the offer of money from BBC Northern Ireland convinced us that the idea might have a series in it. *Give My Head Peace* has completed a third series with a fourth one on the way and is regularly watched by over half the Northern Ireland viewing public.

Tim McGarry
Damon Quinn
Michael McDowell
BELFAST
AUGUST 1999

da

Politics

Sinn Féin Assembly man. For which the DSS stopped his dole money. A livid Da denounced the dole clerk's decision as yet another act of discrimination by an agent of the British Crown. As Da said: 'How can they say being an Assembly man is work. If I do any work, which is denied, it's voluntary and anyway, going up to Stormont once a month and slabbering at the loyalists isn't work at all. In fact it's very pleasurable.'

Fashion

Da has not adapted well to the new Sinn Féin look. He has steadfastly refused to decommission his tweed jacket and duncher. However, following his idol Gerry Adams, he still has a beard 'like Gerry's', has glasses 'like Gerry's', but fear of the dentist, going back to childhood, has prevented him from having his teeth done 'like Gerry's'.

Favourite hobbies

Phoning Gerry, protesting, agitating and being discriminated against.

Origins

Da says that to understand his origins you have to go back eight hundred years to the twelfth century when Ireland, a land of saints and scholars, was subjected to an unprovoked attack by Sasanach English invaders who set themselves the task of destroying the indigenous Celtic culture that had existed for centuries and then . . .

6

da

Q How do you start your day?

A This question is a disgrace. They never even asked me that in Castlereagh.

Q What is your favourite part of the day?

A Teatime. I love cooking. Not doing it, just watching Ma.

Q What is your favourite meal?

A To show my solidarity with the starving Irish peasantry of the nineteenth century I eat potatoes – usually with a twelve-ounce sirloin.

Q What is your favourite book?

A *Da – A Personal History of Ireland in Nine Volumes* which the publishers have declined to print.

Q What is a typical routine?

A First thing every morning I check with Gerry to find out what statements I've made. Then it's all Sinn Féin business – Monday is disband the RUC, Tuesday it's 'Brits out', Wednesday is reroute sectarian marches, Thursday is badminton . . .

Q What is your favourite night-time entertainment?

A Watching my compilation tape of *Gerry Adams Interviews 1970 to Date.*

Q What is your favourite foreign country?

A Libya . . . no sorry, that's not right. I've never been to Libya – don't know why I said that.

*See *Da – A Personal History of Ireland in Nine Volumes*. Da would like interested publishers to note that manuscripts are available on request.

Origins

Ma grew up on the Falls Road. Well when we say 'grew up' we mean grew sideways, as she is well known as the small – or as we prefer to say, 'vertically challenged' – matriarch of Northern Ireland's most dysfunctional family. However, do not let her height – or rather the lack of it – deceive you. Ma is a formidable force when made angry. She is the only person to have scrapped with Red Hand Luke and come off better. As he said at the time, 'That wee woman was scary.'

Ma and Da have never had the most romantic of relationships. Things soured on their honeymoon when Da, with the police looking for him to assist with their inquiries, whisked her away to a remote, freezing farmhouse just outside Dundalk, and whispered tenderly in her ear, 'Don't be talking to nobody.' This set the scene for their life together: Da has been on the run from Ma ever since.

Politics

It was Ma who coined the phrase 'Give My Head Peace', referring to the sectarian strife within her own family. Ma is a one-woman Women's Coalition except, unlike Monica McWilliams, she doesn't have a permanent quivering lip and look like she's about to burst into tears every time she's on camera. She has no time for the antics of Da or Uncle Andy, but if she wasn't married to Da, and if Uncle Andy asked her out, Billy's mother-in-law would be his auntie.

Famous Ma put-downs

Cal

Me and Da have access to secret intelligence.

Ma

Son, if you've any intelligence at all you've kept it hid from me.

*

Da

Aye, damn right the RUC tortured me in Castlereagh.

Ma

Aye, they left you alone in the dark for five minutes.

*

Cal

Them sit-down protests is hard work, you know.

Ma

Not with all the practice you get.

 m^a

Q What's your biggest regret?
A Meeting Da.

Q How do you start your day?
A Badly. I wake up beside Da.

Q Which living person do you most admire?
A It would be between the Pope and Daniel O'Donnell.

Q You have to choose one.
A Well given the devotion he inspires among the faithful worldwide, I'd have to say Daniel O'Donnell.

Q What is your favourite foreign country?
A The only country I got to visit was Libya. Da agreed to take me on a Mediterranean cruise but two weeks in the hold of a trawler crammed in with a lot of crates going from Tripoli to some freezing bay in County Kerry is not what I had in mind.

Q Do you find your height a problem?
A No, I can head butt Da exactly where I want to.

Q Given the difference in their heights, you wouldn't think that Cal was really Da's son.
A What did you say?

Q *Aow!* I didn't mean it. Stop hitting me! Stop hitting me! Don't put me out the window – it's thirteen floors up. Noooooooooooooooooo

two Ceasefires and a Wedding

Transmission date
26 May 1995

We had done it! The BBC had agreed to do our 'Troubles play' spoof for television, it was our big TV break. Then what happens – the IRA calls a ceasefire. The 1994 IRA ceasefire and the subsequent loyalist one brought new challenges and opportunities, a chance for hope and peace and, unfortunately, substantial rewrites for Damon, Tim and myself. But it did give us a damn good title: *Two Ceasefires and a Wedding*.

We decided to bin half the script and base the story on a 'before and after the ceasefire' premise. *Two Ceasefires and a Wedding* was our chance to attack all the clichés of Northern Ireland television. Right from the start we were taking the piss. We opened with the ominous drone of synthesised uilleann pipes as a camera panned over the bleak urban wasteland of Belfast. The caption read: 'Sorry about the droney music and the drab shots of Belfast, but this is a Northern Ireland play.' And all the usual suspects of 'Troubles play' appear – star-crossed lovers: Billy and Emer; bitter loyalist: Uncle Andy; bitter republicans Da and his son Cal (who also had that dodgy English accent); and warm-hearted mother, Ma. We also decided to have a swipe at Daniel Day-Lewis in *In the Name of the Father*, with Paul, a victim of a miscarriage of justice, and his monotonous catch phrase 'I didn't do nothing – I'm innocent.'

Filming proved to be more difficult than we thought. With the coming of the ceasefire you couldn't find a 'Victory to the IRA' mural anywhere in Belfast, so we had to make our own. Also, Damon and myself foolishly agreed to play two British soldiers on patrol around the (actual) peaceline. The locals soon gathered to make their views felt: 'Brits don't walk round corners like that!' and a crowd of kids asked if it was OK to stone us. When it was pointed out that we weren't Brits, just actors, they decided to stone us anyway. Our RUC Land Rover, which was made of plywood, fared much worse. As I play Billy, I'm just glad that my moustache comes off at the end of each day's recording, otherwise I'd never be able to go into a bar.

michael mcdowell

final draft

24/3/95

TWO CEASEFIRES AND A WEDDING

Producer.............................Jackie Hamilton
Director.............................Stephen Butcher
PA...................................Joan Calvert
Designer.............................Andy Johnston
Cameraman............................Bill Browne
Sound................................Gabriel McParland
FM...................................Peter Richie
Make-up..............................Valerie Butler
Costume..............................Ivor Morrow

SCHEDULE

PSC SHOOT:	8, 9 April 1995:	0900-2100
2-CAM SHOOT:	10 April 1995:	0900-2100

STUDIO

SET/LIGHT:	16, 17 April 1995
RECORD:	18 April 1995

CAST: "TWO CEASEFIRES AND A WEDDING"

DA.........................TIM MCGARRY

CAL........................DAMON QUNIN

MA.........................OLIVIA NASH

EMER.......................NUALA McKEEVER

PAUL.......................PETER O'MEARA

UNCLE ANDY.................MARTIN REID

BILLY......................MICHAEL McDOWELL

SOLDIER 1..................DAMON QUINN

SOLDIER 2..................MICHAEL McDOWELL

OFFICER....................MARTIN REID

SARGE......................MARTIN REID

POLICMAN 1.................

POLICMAN 2.................

PHOTOGRAPHER............

CHILDREN...................

NEWSREADER.................

BAND LEADER................

PRISON OFFICER.............

ORGANIST...................OLIVIA NASH

WEDDING QUESTS.............

TWO CEASEFIRES AND A WEDDING

6TH DRAFT

NO MORE DRAFTS!

OPENING CREDITS: 16.03.95

Heavy synthesizer music mixed with lamenting uilean pipes drones heavily. We see the usual mean shots of Belfast: murals, waste ground, dogs urinating, troops on the streets. (STOCK SHOTS)

CAPTION

       THE HOLE IN THE WALL GANG PRESENT......

CAPTION

       TWO CEASEFIRES AND A WEDDING........

CAPTION

       ...... SORRY ABOUT THE DRONEY MUSIC AND THE DRAB SHOTS OF BELFAST BUT THIS IS A NORTHERN IRELAND PLAY

INSERT: WASTELAND SHOT: REVEALS "OLIVIA" PLAYING ORGAN

CAPTION   *ARE WE GOING TO DRESS HER IN BLACK SCOTTISH WIDOWS GEAR?*

       BELFAST 30TH AUGUST 1994.... BEFORE THE CEASEFIRE

SCENE 1: EXT. "DIVIS TOWER". DAY FOR DUSK. (DAY ONE)

DURING THE LAST CAPTION WE FOCUS IN ON DIVIS TOWER. FX: CLOUDS/RAIN - POSSIBLE SUBLIMINAL FLASHES OF DRACULA CASTLE (STOCK SHOT). CUT TO INT. 47A DIVIS TOWER.

SCENE 2: INT. KITCHEN. 47A DIVIS TOWER DUSK/NIGHT

DARK ROOM LIT POORLY. A COOLIE LAMP PRODUCES THE LITTLE, SINISTER LIGHT. DA AND CAL TWO IRA MEN ARE SITTING AT A BAR PINE TABLE.

DA:
Right, lets call this meeting of the Lower

Falls Brigade of the IRA to order. Roll

call..... Cal!

CAL:
Here daddy!

DA:
Good then we're all here. Now, before we

start, did you do that job I asked you to do?

CAL:
Yes daddy, it's primed to go off any

second now.

C/A KETTLE BOILING

DA: well
Cal, you make the tea and I'll tell you about the

new consignment I got in this morning.

CAL:
What is it Daddy? More Libyan arms?

Czech semtex?

DA:
Na....hobnobs......chocolate ones.

(CAL STARTS LAUGHING EVILLY)

CAL:
What do you think of my evil laugh,

Daddy?

DA:
Not bad - but have you tried it like this?

DA STARTS LONG, MANIC LAUGH

CAL:
Very good- but why do WE have to have a

crazed psychotic laugh anyway?

DA:
Because we're evil godfathers of terrorism.

How many IRA films have you have in.

Now get on with it - will you.

BOTH LAUGH MANICALLY

SCENE 3:   INT.   LIVING ROOM 47A DIVIS
TOWER. DUSK/NIGHT

MA AND EMER ARE IN THE FLAT. WE HEAR
CLANNAD - THE THEME FROM HARRY'S GAME.
MA IS DUSTING THE FRONT ROOM.

MA:
Turn that bloody racket off.

EMER:
Sorry Ma.

MA:
Its bad enough living on the Falls Road

without you playing that record to remind

us...... God I'm depressed.

EMER:
What is it Ma? The 25 years of violence?

The unemployment? The poverty?

MA:
Aye that and the weather.

EMER:
Do you think it'll ever change?

MA:
Well they say it's going to brighten

up later on.

EMER:
No the Troubles Ma. Do you think we'll

ever see peace?

MA:
Naw. You know what I'd like to do? I'd like to take the lot of them the IRA the UDA and put them on an island and let them shoot each other all they want.

EMER:
Ma this is an island and that's what they're doing.

SCENE 4: INT. KITCHEN 47A DIVIS TOWER. DUSK/NIGHT.

CAL:
Daddy, there's a disturbing rumour going round that there's going to be a ceasefire.

DA:
You're right Cal, there will be a ceasefire, —— just as soon as we've driven every last Brit out of this island!

CAL:
So it won't be for quite a while then, Daddy?

DA:
By the time this is over, your ~~Northern~~ Belfast ~~Ireland~~ accent will be perfect.

CAL: That long? **(THEY BOTH LAUGH)**

ENTER WOMAN WHO FLICKS ON THE LIGHTS TO REVEAL THAT DA AND CAL ARE, IN FACT, SITTING IN THE KITCHEN OF 47A DIVIS TOWER

MA:
Look, do you have to hold your IRA meetings in my kitchen? It's very anti-social. Why don't you join the rest of your family in the living room?

DA:
We can't hold our IRA meetings with the TV on. Cal loses interest in the struggle once Noel's House Party starts.

MA:
You're leading that son of yours astray.

DA:
Well, at least I'm taking an interest in him. He could be out in the streets falling in with the wrong sorts if I hadn't got him into the IRA.

MA:
Aye but what about the rest of your children you've them terrorised. You tarred and feathered Dympna.

DA:
Have you seen the phone bill?

SCENE 4A: INT. LIVING ROOM

MA:
You've given Una 24 hours to leave the country.

DA:
She forgot to video The Quiet Man!

MA:
And there's nothing worse than what you did to your son Paul.

DA:
I never laid a finger on Paul.

MA:
Holiday in England, you said. He'd broaden his horizons, you said. Group activities, you said. Free accommodation, you said. Fifteen years of free accommodation at Her Majesty's pleasure he had for something you did!

DA:
Eh...

EMER:
He never got over his time in jail - scarred he is.

DA:
That's no excuse for the way he gets on.
No matter what you say to him he's like a
stuck record. I didn't do it. I'm innocent.

DA:
The Troubles in this country have nothing
to do with religion...it's the Prods...you
couldn't like them.

(ENTER PAUL)

Should he be wearing 70's gear?

PAUL:
What are you accusing me of now?

MA:
Nothing Paul.

PAUL:
Cos I didn't do it...whatever it is I'm

innocent.

MA:
Paul will you give over... you're driving

everybody nuts!

PAUL:
No I'm not. I'm not driving anybody nuts.

I'm innocent. I didn't do it. I'm innocent.

Tasteless but funny

MA:
Look what you've done to your family and

all because of some stupid war over

religion.

SCENE 6: INT. LIVING ROOM. UNCLE ANDY'S. DAY.

WE OPEN WITH CLOSE SHOT OF UNCLE ANDY. UNCLE ANDY: MID-50'S - KITSCH TENDENCIES - RED VELVET JACKET BEHIND DOOR. WHEN WE FIRST SEE UNCLE ANDY HE IS DRESSED LIKE ANDY TYRIE WITH TINTED GLASSES AND A MEXICAN DROOPING MOUSTACHE. HE WEARS A LEATHER JACKET AND IS READING "COMBAT".

SHOULD HE BE AN ELVIS FAN?

UNCLE ANDY:
Billy I'm not sectarian. The trouble with this country's not religion ... it's the bloody Taigs. You couldn't like them.

CAMERA SWINGS OVER TO BILLY WHO IS PUTTING AN RUC UNIFORM ON.

BILLY:
Uncle Andy, you're talking rubbish. Just because you're a Catholic doesn't make you a bad person...some Italians and Spanish are very nice people.

DO I HAVE TO WEAR A MOUSTACHE?

UNCLE ANDY:
Why did you join the police Billy? Bringing shame on me. I'm a laughing stock down at the Loyalist Kneebreakers Club.

BILLY:
You know why I joined the police Uncle Andy. Open your eyes! Take a look at the state this country's in! This was something I had to do.

UNCLE ANDY:
Why Billy?

BILLY:
For the money, of course. Sure I've been loaded every since.

UNCLE ANDY:
If it was money you wanted, I could have got you a start in the UDA. You could have had 20 video shops by now.

BILLY:
I wanted to do more with my life then work in a video shop.

UNCLE ANDY:
Work? All you'd have to do is collect.

BILLY:
So that's your ambition for me - running a video racket?

UNCLE ANDY:
Sorry - you're right. Tell you what, I'll cut you into the drugs.

BILLY:
No!

UNCLE ANDY:
Building sites?

BILLY:
I'm off.

UNCLE ANDY:
Why, are you working tonight?

BILLY:
Have to. There's rumours of an IRA

ceasefire and if that happens, it could be a

very serious situation.

UNCLE ANDY:
What? Ulster sold out? Civil War!

BILLY:
No, we'll lose our overtime. And if there's

peace it could be even worse, redundancies.

UNCLE ANDY:
So where are you off to tonight?

BILLY:
I'm on harassment duty on the Falls Road.

UNCLE ANDY:
Harassment me arse. Knowing you you'll

probably fall in love with some Fenian

called Emer and get this family mixed up in

a love across the barricades romance

involving the Provos, loyalist paramilitaries

and God knows what else, leading to the

inevitable tragic denouement.

BILLY: DID YOU
What?   GOT THAT PLOT?

UNCLE ANDY:
You heard.

SCENE 7: EXT. FALLS ROAD. DAY

2 BRITISH SOLDIERS ARE ON PATROL WALKING PAST PRE-CEASEFIRE REPUBLICAN MURALS.

WHERE ARE WE DOING THIS?

SOLDIER 1: *WILL THERE BE PROTECTION?*
I'm on patrol last night - only out 5 minutes and would you believe it - shooting incident!

SOLDIER 2:
What? IRA sniper?

SOLDIER 1:
No, that bloody dipstick Corporal Jones.

SOLDIER 2:
Yeah, I heard about that - still I suppose to be fair to Jonesy, it could have been an IRA car.

SOLDIER 1:
IRA cars do not have "Just Married" on the back of them.

SOLDIER 2:
Oh dear - I wouldn't fancy being him. He's in trouble now. Going to charge him, are they?

SOLDIER 1:
No, it's alright, we got the road block up just in time for the police arriving.

(ENTER AN OFFICER)

OFFICER:
Listen chaps, between ourselves apparently there's a suspicious package behind that hedge. Would you mind awfully checking it out.

SOLDIER 1:
Off you go Dave.

SOLDIER 2:
What do you mean? I did the last one.

SOLDIER 1:
No you didn't.

SOLDIER 2:
Yes I did. I took care of that suspect keg.

SOLDIER 1:
You drank that suspect keg!

OFFICER:
Go on - the both of you.

THEY RELUCTANTLY WALK 5 YARDS TOWARDS A HEDGE WHICH IS 50 YARDS AWAY. THEY CRANE THEIR NECKS TOWARDS THE HEDGE THEN TURN AWAY.

SOLDIER 1:
No - it looks alright Sir.

SOLDIER 2:
But I wouldn't get too close to it.

SCENE 8: INT. RUC LANDROVER. DAY.

SARGE, 2 POLICEMEN AND BILLY ARE SITTING AT THE BACK OF THE LANDROVER.

SARGE:
...So after 8 hours of interrogation, we finally

got Mad Dog McClatchey to talk.

you.

BILLY:
What did he say?

SARGE:
Ah!!! Stop hitting me! **(LAUGHS)**

So it's 47A Divis Tower again!

Have you been here before, Billy?

BILLY:
No.

SARGE:
Well here's what we do. We knock the door

once kick it down, then we all charge our way in,

rip up the floorboards, smash up all the furniture

and ornaments, generally wreck the place and,

eh, there's something else. What is it? It's on

the tip of my tongue...

BILLY:
Search it?

SARGE:
Oh, aye, **(LAUGHS)** and search it.

SCENE 9: INT.   LIVING ROOM. 47A DIVIS TOWER. DAY.

MA, DA, CAL AND EMER ARE IN THE FRONT ROOM. PAUL IS TRYING TO WATCH TV. MA IS IRONING 2 BALACLAVAS.   AS THE SCENE PROGRESSES, SHE IRONS A BOILER SUIT AND A TRICOLOUR. SOUND FX: CELL BLOCK H COD DIALOGUE B/G.

MA:
So I want to know - is there going to be a

ceasefire or not?

DA:
In the words of Patrick Pearse in 1916, as he was

being led out to be shot by the British, "No, not

today thank you".

MA:
But this never ending spiralling cycle of violence

has got to stop.

DA:
Why? what's wrong with it?

MA:
It's never-ending. It's spiralling and it's cyclical,

that's what's wrong with it.

DA:
As well as being a bloody cliche.

MA:
It's destroying this country.

PAUL:
Will yous keep it down - I'm trying to watch my favourite programme here.

EMER:
You shouldn't be watching Prisoner Cell Block H, it only reminds you.

CAL:
Paul, why don't you join the Provos like me and Daddy? It's great fun.

PAUL:
You must be joking - it's because of the IRA that I was put in jail for 15 years for something I did not do!

CAL:
Sure if you joined the Provos you could get 15 years for something you did do.

LOUD KNOCK ON THE DOOR

EMER:
What's that?

SOUND OF THE DOOR BEING SMASHED DOWN, SEVERAL POLICEMEN INCLUDING BILLY ENTER AND START SMASHING UP THE FLAT.

DA:
Looks like our regular police raid.

SARGE:
Right Constable Williams wreck the bathroom.

Constable Robinson smash up the bedrooms ....

Ach daddy, how's it going?

DA:
Not bad Sammy. How's the Mrs.?

MA:
Yis are early tonight. Do yis want a wee cup of tea now or after yis finish?

SARGE:
Better have it now cos we'll be wrecking the kitchen in a minute.

EXIT MA

COP 2 PRODUCES PLUG AND FLEX

SARGE:
Where can he plug this in?

DA:
Over there, son.

COP 2 PLUGS IN THE LEAD TO THE SOCKET. WE NOW SEE THAT THE PIECE OF ELECTRICAL EQUIPMENT IS A CHAINSAW. HE STARTS UP THE CHAINSAW AND STARTS CUTTING UP THE FURNITURE.

How are we going to use a chainsaw on set?

DA:
See the match last night?

SARGE:
Aye, yis were robbed. Constable Robinson make sure you're not careful with that drill. Constable Black take the names. Any sign of that kanga hammer?

BILLY:
Ok, names!

DA:
DADDY

CAL:
CAL

PAUL:
I'm innocent. I didn't do it.

SARGE:
Arrest him!

PAUL:
I didn't do it, I'm innocent.

BILLY:
And your name is?

EMER:
EMER

BILLY:
That's a beautiful name, Emer.

BILLY AND EMER ARE FILMED IN SOFT FOCUS. THE NOISE OF THE COMMOTION AROUND THEM FADES AND WE HEAR ROMANTIC MUSIC.

EMER:
What's your name?

BILLY:
Billy, I think I'm in love with you Emer.

EMER:
I love you too Billy.

BILLY:
Emer - Do you think a Protestant and a Taig.....and a Catholic can love each other?

EMER:
Yes Billy I do.

BILLY:
They'll try to stop us with their hate.

EMER:
I know - but love conquers everything.

THE MUSIC FADES DOWN AND WE RETURN TO THE SCENE OF MAYHEM. PAUL IS BEING DRAGGED AWAY SHOUTING THAT HE IS INNOCENT. MEANWHILE EMER AND BILLY ARE WAVING ROMANTICALLY AT EACH OTHER AND BLOWING KISSES. THE POLICE ARE PACKING UP. "OUR TUNE" MUSIC.

SARGE:
Right I think that's everything.

DA:
Would you sign the compensation form.

SARGE:
No problem.

HE SIGNS THE FORM. ENTER MA WITH TRAY FULL OF TEA THINGS.

MA:
You forgot about this.

SARGE:
Oh, sorry.

COP 1 SMASHES UP CROCKERY ON THE TRAY WITH A TRUNCHEON

SARGE:
Right see you next week hopefully.

DA:
All the best, Sammy.

THE POLICE EXIT - BILLY AND EMER WAVE TO EACH OTHER.

DA:
There's only one thing I hate more than Brits, and

that's peelers.

SCENE 10: EXT. DIVIS TOWER. DAY (DAY THREE)

FX: CLOUDS/RAIN. DAY FOR DUSK

SCENE 11: INT. LIVING ROOM 47A DIVIS
TOWER. DAY
CAPTION - "AUGUST 31ST 1994"

DADDY AND CAL ARE DRESSING IN
PARAMILITARY TYPE GEAR PREPARING TO GO
ON A "JOB". MA IS IRONING A LARGE CLOTH.
WE DON'T KNOW WHAT IT IS. EMER
MEANWHILE IS TALKING TO BILLY ON THE
PHONE.

EMER:
Oh Billy - It's lovely to hear from you...how did

you get my number? You went and got my file

out? How romantic... I love you too Billy.

Billy....

DA:
(TO CAL)   Semtex?

CAL:
Check.

DA:
Grappling hooks?

CAL:
Check.

DA:
10p for the phone to claim responsibility?

CAL:
Check.

MA:
What are yous doing?

CAL:
We're going to spring Paul out of jail Mammy.

MA:
You'll do no such thing - let me get Paul out my

way. I've started a campaign.

SHE HOLD UP CLOTH TO REVEAL SLOGAN
"FREE THE BELFAST ONE".

MA:
"Free the Belfast One"

CAL AND DADDY HEAD FOR THE DOOR

DA:
That'll take 15 years. Cal and I will have him out

in 15 seconds. (TO CAL) Come on, we're

wasting time.

EMER:
Bye, bye, love.

SHE PUTS THE PHONE DOWN AND SITS IN
FRONT OF THE TV WATCHING IT

MA: (MOVING TO THE FRONT DOOR)
You're going nowhere; your violence and hate has

to stop.

DA:
The violence will never end!

EMER: **(EXCITED)**
Daddy - the news.

DA:
The Republican movement will never surrender to

the British oppressor - Never!

EMER:
Daddy!

DA:
Do you think we have resisted British imperialism

for 800 years just to stop now!

EMER:
Daddy - Look! **(SHE POINTS TO THE TV)**

DA:
The armed struggle continues!

JULIAN SEATED TO CAMERA

TV NEWSREADER:
Here, within the last 2 minutes the IRA has

announced a complete cessation of military

operations. These are the scenes on the Falls

Road as Gerry Adams told his fans!

WE SEE ORIGINAL REACTION FOOTAGE OF ANNOUNCEMENT. WE CUT TO SHOTS OF CROWDS DANCING AT NOTTING HILL, MARDI GRAS, BEATLES CONCERT, AND A SHOT OF A CROWD DOING THE MEXICAN WAVE. WE SEE A SHOT OF A MAORI WAR DANCE. WE CUT TO A SCENE AT ST. PETER'S SQUARE WITH BELLS PEALING. THEN SCENES FROM THE COLLAPSE OF THE BERLIN WALL AND FINALLY A SCENE FROM WOODSTOCK.

DADDY FREEZES - HE IS HORRIFIED.

SCENE 12: INT. UNCLE ANDY'S HOUSE. DAY.

UNCLE ANDY IS WATCHING TELEVISION. HE IS STUNNED. BILLY IS WITH HIM - HE LOOKS DISAPPOINTED.

UNCLE ANDY:
Peace? - I don't like the sound of that Billy.

BILLY:
Neither do I. There goes my job and I've just

bought a Merc.

SCENE 13: EXT: FALLS ROAD. DAYTIME.

THE SAME BRITISH SOLDIERS AS BEFORE ARE RELAXED; THEY HAVE FLOWERS IN THEIR GUNS AND ARE OSTENTATIOUSLY HUGGING YOUNG CHILDREN IN FRONT OF A CAMERAMAN.

SOLDIER 1:
Yeah, It's great news.

SOLDIER 2:
I'm really glad it's over....Is that enough Sir?

OFFICER:
Yeah, alright, I think we can finish with the kids

now.

SOLDIER 1:
OK, clear off you little brats! (HE CUFFS A CHILD)

SCENE 14:   INT: LIVING ROOM. 47A DIVIS TOWER. DAY

CAL AND DADDY ARE STANDING IN FRONT OF THE TV. DADDY HAS FROZEN. HE IS STILL HORRIFIED AND UNABLE TO SPEAK.

CAL:
We could always say we just didn't see the news

daddy.

SCENE 15   EXT: CAVE HILL. DAY. (DAY FOUR: FORTNIGHT LATER)

LATER. BILLY AND EMER ARE SITTING ON THE CAVE HILL, HAVING A ROMANTIC PICNIC. BILLY IS IN UNIFORM.

EMER:
Oh, Billy, it's so good to be out in the country.

BILLY:
Yes, Emer darling.

EMER:
And in a way our love is a beacon of hope for a

new era of peace in our land...

BILLY: (SLIGHTLY MORE INTERESTED IN OTHER THINGS)
Yes that's right.

EMER:
We're a symbol of reconciliation and hope,

Catholic and Protestant coming together....

BILLY:
Yeah, I'm all for that.

SMUTTY! SMUTTY! SMUTTY! WILL WE GET IT THROUGH.

EMER:
Living in harmony and peace without fear of

violence - a new dawn for us, a new future for

the whole of Northern Ireland...

BILLY:
Emer, no harm to you, but I'm on duty in half an

hour.

THEY EMBRACE PASSIONATELY

EMER:
Billy, do you not think you should wear some

protection, just in case.

BILLY:
Right enough.

BILLY PUTS ON FLAK JACKET AND THEY GET DOWN TO IT. CAMERA PANS OFF TO REVEAL GV BELFAST "OLIVIA" F/G PLAYING ORGAN.

SCENE 16: INT. KITCHEN. 47A DIVIS TOWER. DUSK.
(DAY FOUR)

DADDY IS ON THE PHONE. HE IS WEARING A VERY EXPENSIVE LOOKING SUIT.

DA:
Yes Gerry, I know that - and I do accept the new

situation Gerry, but it would have been nice to be

told......you knew I'd be upset? I was more upset

to hear about it on the TV Gerry! I am the

commander of the Lower Falls Brigade - it would

have been nice to hear it from you rather than the

British Broadcasting Corporation!!

SCENE 16A: INT. LIVING ROOM. DUSK.

DADDY MOVES INTO THE LIVING ROOM. IT IS STUFFED FULL OF ARMS, BOXES OF SEMTEX AND OTHER PARAMILITARY PARAPHERNALIA. CAL HAS PAINTED A POSTER "A JUST PEACE NOW" AND IS BUSY WORKING ON ANOTHER ONE WHICH READS "DEMILITARISE NOW".

CAL:
Have I spelt demilitarise right Daddy?

DA: (HOLDING DICTIONARY)
Yeah, I think so.

CAL:
I preferred "Brits Out". It had a much better ring to it.

DA:
Well, Gerry says it's the same thing.

CAL:
Nice suit Daddy.

DA:
Thanks, it's the new image. Gerry says armalites are out, Armanis are in.

CAL:
Well, I don't agree with it Daddy!

DA:
What?

CAL:
You get a much better cut with Versace. (CAL PRODUCES SUIT ON HANGER).

ENTER MA

MA:
Well my God! You've a right cheek, demilitarise now!

DA: (CHECKING A PISTOL)
It's time to take the gun out of Irish politics - isn't that right Cal?

CAL:
I couldn't agree more; but where are we going to store them?   BEST JOKE IN THE SCRIPT.

MA:
So you're all for peace now?

DA:
We were always for peace! What do you think we had 25 years of armed struggle for?

MA:
Get that mess cleared away.

Emer's bringing her new boyfriend home for dinner.

DA: (TO CAL)
Gerry's explained it to me. The struggle is entering a new phase, where we have to build a just peace based on self determination for the Irish people and parity of esteem for all sections of the community, Catholics, Protestant and dissenter.

ENTER EMER AND BILLY. BILLY IS STILL DRESSED IN HIS RUC UNIFORM

EMER:
Mammy, Daddy, this is Billy.

DA: (LEAPING FROM HIS SEAT)
Cal! It's a peeler! Quick where's my gun!

HE PICKS UP A CUSHION AND RETRIEVES A GUN FROM UNDER IT.

IS HE GOING TO POINT THE GUN AT BILLY?

MA:
Ah, Ah, Ah, (TAKE DADDY'S GUN AWAY) What did Gerry say, the gun is now out of Irish politics.

BILLY: (AWKWARDLY TO DADDY)
How do you do?

(HE SWEEPS AN ORNAMENT OF THE MANTLEPIECE WITH HIS TRUNCHEON).

Sorry, force of habit.

EMER:
You must remember him Daddy - He's the one who was in wrecking our house and arrested Paul.

DADDY LOOKS APPALLED

DA:
Ah, ... Right.

DADDY FAINTS

SCENE 17: EXT: FALLS ROAD. DAY.
(DAY FIVE)

CAL AND DADDY ARE WALKING UP THE FALLS ROAD PAST POST-CEASEFIRE MURALS.

DA:
If only she'd brought him home a week ago we could have....

CAL:
We are still allowed to do kneecappings Daddy.

DA:
He hasn't committed any anti-social acts has he?

CAL:
Well he is a policeman.

THEY WALK PAST THE 3 BRITISH SOLDIERS WE SAW EARLIER. NOW THEY ARE LOOKING VERY BORED. THEY HAVE LENT THEIR GUNS AGAINST A WALL AND ARE SITTING ON THE PAVEMENT. ONE OF THEM IS PLAYING A GAMEBOY. ANOTHER ONE IS STANDING CHEWING BUBBLE GUM AND PLAYING WITH A YO-YO.

SCENE 18 INT: UNCLE ANDY'S HOUSE. DAY.

UNCLE ANDY IS SITTING POLISHING HIS COLLECTION OF SUNGLASSES WHEN BILLY AND EMER ENTER.

BILLY:
Uncle Andy...I want you to meet somebody.

UNCLE ANDY:
Ach, is this your new girl?

BILLY:
Aye.

UNCLE ANDY:
Come on in love.

EMER:
Thanks.

UNCLE ANDY:
Sit down, do you want a wee cup of tea? Ach

you will, you will.

BILLY:
Uncle Andy this is....

UNCLE ANDY:
A wee cup of tea and some biscuits

BILLY:
This is Emer.

UNCLE ANDY:
Get that Fenian bitch out of my house!

BILLY:
But Uncle Andy - There's peace now.

UNCLE ANDY:
So? Does that mean I've to like Fenians.

BILLY:
Uncle Andy - You don't understand.

UNCLE ANDY:
Of course I don't understand I'm a 2 dimensional

character. A dyed in wool, stereotypical, loyalist

bigot. I don't understand until something terrible

happens and I realise the tragedy my hate has

caused cf Romeo and Juliet the Act 5 Scene 3.

BILLY:
Oh, I see.

POOR MARTT IS GETTING ALL THE BEST LINES.

UNCLE ANDY:
But until then - Get that Fenian bitch out of my

house!

SCENE 19: INT: LIVING ROOM. 47A DIVIS TOWER. DUSK
(DAY SIX)

LIVING ROOM DA, MA AND CAL ARE SEATED. MA IS READING A "NORTHERN WOMAN" FEATURING - "BERNADETTE McALISKEY ON FASHION". CAL IS READING AN PHOBLACHT WITH THE HEADLINE "GIVE PEACE A CHANCE". DA IS READING "THE LIFE OF MAHATMA GHANDI"

CAL:
What are you reading Daddy?

DA:
Gerry lent it to me. It's the life of Mahatma Ghandi. Apparently he got rid of the Brits without firing a single shot.

CAL:
Bombed them out did he?

DA:
I've read it twice and I'm still not sure how he did it.

CAL:
What are we going to do about our Emer and this peeler Daddy.

DA:
Nothing. I've been thinking about it. It's just a phase she's going through. It'll be over in a couple of weeks.

ENTER BILLY AND EMER WITH A BOTTLE OF CHAMPAGNE

EMER:
Daddy. Great news. Billy has asked me to marry him and I've said yes.   Daddy?

BILLY UNCORKS THE CHAMPAGNE.   DA STARES STRAIGHT AHEAD COMPLETELY SHOCKED

CAL: (TO DADDY)
A peeler in the family. What would Ghandi have done?

DA: (TURNS SLOWLY TO CAL)
...He'd have shot him.

BILLY HANDS DA A GLASS OF CHAMPAGNE AND PUTS HIS ARM AROUND HIM. IT IS A LITLE LATER.

BILLY:
There you go, Da! So, Ma, it's definitely going to be a church wedding.

MA:
I'll speak to Father O'Brien and.....

BILLY:
No, Ma, Presbyterian.

MA:
But I thought you wanted a church wedding.

BILLY:
We're going to have a big reception and we're got the RUC band for free. Now that there's peace, they do weddings, christenings, the heap.

CAL:
Do they know "The men behind the wire"?

BILLY:
They should do, they put most of them there.

(HE LAUGHS, NOBODY ELSE DOES) And they do a brilliant rendition of "The Sash". You'll love it. It's a calypso version...eh any chance of a beer there brother?

DA STANDS UP.

DA:
Army Council meeting Cal.

SCENE 20: INT: KITCHEN. 47A DIVIS TOWER. DUSK .

KITCHEN CAL IS GETTING BEERS OUT OF THE FRIDGE. DA IS DIALLING A NUMBER ON THE TELEPHONE

CAL:
A nice enough fellow in his own way daddy. But a peeler nonetheless.

DA:
Hello, Gerry...yeah, I appreciate I've got you out of a meeting with the Taoiseach in Dublin but I just want a bit of clarification here. Just how complete and total is this cessation of violence.

SCENE 21: INT. LIVING ROOM. UNCLE ANDY'S HOUSE. DAY.

UNCLE ANDY:

SHOULD THAT BE EATING A FRY? — ON SECOND THOUGHTS IM A VEGETARIAN

You're going to marry that Fenian Billy? I'd rather kill myself than see you marry a taig!

BILLY:
Is religion that important to you Uncle Andy?

UNCLE ANDY:
No, you're right, I'd rather kill you than see you married to a Taig. How could you betray the Protestant loyalist people? For years we stood our ground, in the last ditch with our backs to the wall against the Fenian hordes. Our forefathers did not fight in the trenches of the River Boyne for you to dance on the grave of our way of life.

BILLY:
Uncle Andy you're so consumed with hatred you're mixing your metaphors... open your eyes and take a look around you... where have all the years of violence got us? We've got to provide a better future for our children, where it doesn't matter if you're a Protestant or a Catholic. Where kids can learn to play together.

That's why me and Emer have to get married. To show that there's a better future.

UNCLE ANDY:
She's pregnant then?

BILLY:
Aye.

UNCLE ANDY:
Billy....I'm begging you... don't do it.

BILLY:
What are you afraid of?

UNCLE ANDY:
I'm afraid of you showing that a Catholic and Protestant can love each other....I'm afraid of the Troubles ending... I'm afraid of getting no more parts as a bitter loyalist in crap Northern Ireland films and plays.

OUR ALTOR MATES WILL LOVE THIS!

BILLY:
You'll just have to learn to act.

UNCLE ANDY:
I'm warning you, Billy, some of the lads in the UDA aren't a bit happy about this wedding.

BILLY:
So what! They're not invited.

SCENE 22: EXT. CRUMLIN ROAD JAIL. DAY. (DAY SEVEN)

ESTABLISHING SHOT CRUMLIN ROAD JAIL COAL LORRY DRIVES PAST WITH OLIVIA ON BACK PLAYING ORGAN.
CAPTION(?): CRUMLIN ROAD PRISON FOR THE INNOCENT.

SCENE 23: INT. PRISON CELL. DAY.

PAUL IS SEATED LOOKING AGITATED. CELL DOOR OPENS. PRISON OFFICER ENTERS

PRISON OFFICER:
Good news, Paul, you're being releiased.

PAUL:
THANK GOD!

PRISON OFFICER:
Only joking you've got visitors. I love my job.

ENTER BILLY AND EMER

PAUL:
I'm innocent. I didn't do it.

BILLY:
Hi, Paul.

PAUL: (TO BILLY)
Who are you, are you my lawyer.

EMER:
No sorry, actually Paul he's the policeman who

arrested you.

PAUL:
You know I didn't do nothing. I'm innocent.

BILLY:
I know that. Listen I've got some great news for

you.

PAUL:
I've won my appeal.

BILLY:
I'm going to marry your sister, and we'd like you

to be my best man, none of my mates or family

will do it so Emer suggested you.

PAUL:
But I'm innocent. I'm not signing nothing.

BILLY:
You don't have to sign anything. You just have

to say a few words.

PAUL:
I'm not confessing to nothing.

BILLY:
If you do you'll get a day out on compassionate

leave.

PAUL:
A day out on compassionate leave for something

I did not do.

SCENE 24: EXT. FRONT GATES OF CRUMLIN ROAD JAIL. DAY.

BILLY AND EMER LEAVE JAIL. DURING THEIR DIALOGUE WE HEAR THE CRIES OF PAUL SHOUTING "I'M INNOCENT", "I DIDN'T DO IT", "I MIGHT HAVE BEEN THERE, I DON'T KNOW". "STOP HITTING ME".

EMER:
I think that cheered him up Billy.

BILLY:
That's good.

THEY WALK DOWN THE STREET HAND IN HAND PAST BRIT 1 AND BRIT 2 OF THE 'BORED BRITS'. THEY ARE STANDING CASUALLY ABOUT THE FOOTPATH, THEIR RIFLES LEFT CARELESSLY AGAINST THE WALL.

SOLDIER 1:
I spy with my little eye something beginning with

'R'.

SOLDIER 2:
Road.

SOLDIER 1:
Yeah.

SOLDIER 2:
I spy with my little eye something beginning with

'C'.

SOLDIER 1:
Cars.

give my head peace

Michael and Damon as fearsome Brits

Da and Cal can't decide what to give Emer as a wedding present.
A baseball bat perhaps?

SOLDIER 2:
Yeah. That's right......God I'm bored. It's more

dangerous on a Sunday in Surbiton than it is

here.

THE OFFICER APPROACHES

OFFICER:
Right, listen up men. I've just heard there's been

a very serious incident on the Falls Road.

SOLDIER 1:
What, a riot?

OFFICER:
No, chap's dropped his wallet and we need all

available personnel to help him look for it. Now

here's the plan. Company 'B' are fanning out on

a recce and will rendezvous with us at

Andersonstown Police Station....

SOLDIER 2:
Boring!

SOLDIER 1:
Yeah, c'mon Sir, we're soldiers. We need

thrills and excitement. We need to live on our

nerves.

OFFICER:
Okay, well if you're that bored how about I

volunteer us for a transfer to Bosnia.

SOLDIER 1:
Gents wallet you say sir?

SOLDIER 2:
What's it look like sir?

SCENE 25: INT. LIVING ROOM. FLAT 47A DIVIS TOWER. DUSK.

CAL, BILLY, MA AND EMER ARE SEATED. CAL IS READING AN PHOBLACT. THE HEADLINE IS 'ALL YOU NEED IS LOVE'. BILLY IS WATCHING A RANGERS V CELTIC MATCH ON TELEVISION. INSERT RANGERS V CELTIC FOOTAGE. HE IS WEARING A RANGERS SCARF AND CLUTCHING A CAN OF BEER. RANGERS HAVE JUST SCORED AND BILLY JUMPS UP CHEERING. DA IS SITTING ON A HARD SEAT SULKING, AND TRYING TO READ A BOOK CALLED "A BEGINNER'S GUIDE TO PACIFISM".

BILLY:
Yes! One nil! It's one nil to Rangers Da! Celtic's getting a hammering!

DA PEERS OVER HIS BOOK IRRITABLY

MA: (TO EMER)
Don't get me wrong, I'm glad there's peace. But there's some things you miss about the Troubles.

EMER:
What Ma?

MA:
Ach, the cost of living's gone up. You remember your daddy used to say, 'Don't be going to that shop to buy me a suit till after Wednesday'... and sure enough come Thursday there'd be 50% off for smoke damage.

EMER:
Aye, and you remember everytime I had a hangover I used to phone in and say I'll be a hour late, there's a bomb scare in our street.

MA:
Yeah, and every now and again your Da and Cal would get lifted by the police and we'd get a break from them.

EMER:
Yes, but think about all the foreign tourists that'll be coming now. Germans, Americans...

MA:
Free Staters. At least when your Da was fighting for a United Ireland, we didn't have to put up with a lot of southerners swamping the place.

EMER:
Ma, do you think Daddy will ever accept Billy.

MA:
Ach, aye, in a couple of months time they'll be going to the football together.

BILLY JUMPS UP

BILLY:
Yes! Two nil! Yes!

DA GETS UP AND LEAVES - DISGUSTED.

MA:
Of course, they'll be in separate terraces.

BILLY:
Rangers! Rangers! Rangers! Rangers!

(STARTS DANCING AROUND CAL SINGING)

we are, we are, we are the Billy boys. Da! we're

stuffing you! Any chance of another beer DA!

SCENE 26: INT. KITCHEN. 47A DIVIS TOWER. DUSK.

DA IS ON THE TELEPHONE

DA:
I know that. I know that Gerry. I know you're in

the middle of a meeting in the White House... I

know the peace process is at a very sensitive

stage... I know the eyes of the world are on us...

I know that any breach of the ceasefire could

have disastrous consequences for the future of

these islands - but you don't have a fucking

peeler sitting in your front room supporting

Glasgow Rangers!

THERE'S NO FUCKING WAT WE'LL
GET THE
DA SLAMS RECEIVER DOWN. 'FUCKING'
THROUGH!

BILLY ENTERS.

BILLY:
What about that beer, Da?

DA:
There's none left, son!

BILLY:
Well, I'll nip out for some.

**BILLY EXITS SINGING 3-NIL, 3-NIL.
CAL ENTERS.**

DA:
Cal, this ceasefire will be the death

of me.

(DA EXITS)

CAL: (TO HIMSELF)
Well I'm not going to stand idly by anymore. I'm

going to make this a wedding to remember.

SCENE 27:   INT. LIVING ROOM. 47A DIVIS TOWER. DUSK.

CAL RE-ENTERS.

CAL:
Mammy. Do you know where my timing devices

are?

MA: (ROLLS EYES)
They're on the shelf in the false cavity

behind the cupboard.

CAL: (REMEMBERING)
Ah, that's right... and what about the Mercury tilt

switch?

MA:
In the hole underneath the cooker.

CAL:
Right   (EXITS)

MA:
And take that semtex out of the fridge. I nearly

iced a cake with it last night.

SCENE 28: EXT. FALLS ROAD. DAY.
(DAY EIGHT)

THE BORED BRITS ARE PLAYING CHARADES.
BRIT 1 AND 2 ARE SAT ON A WALL. THE
SERGEANT IS MIMING A MOVIE CAMERA

SOLDIER 1:
Film.

OFFICER: (NODS, THEN HOLDS UP THREE
            FINGERS)

SOLDIER 2:
Three words.

(OFFICER HOLDS UP TWO FINGERS)

SOLDIER 1:
Second word.

(OFFICER MIMES CRYING)

SOLDIERS 1 & 2:
The Crying Game!

(BILLY AND EMER WALK PAST HOLDING
HANDS)

EMER:
Oh Billy, I can't wait until tomorrow. We'll finally

be man and wife. We'll be a shining example of

the new way forward for our two divided

communities.

BILLY:
Aye. Did you tell your Da you're pregnant yet?

EMER:
Yes I did. I think he wants a boy

because he went straight out and

bought a baseball bat.

SCENE 29: INT. KITCHEN. 47A DIVIS TOWER. DUSK.

DA IS ON THE TELEPHONE.

DA:
Gerry, I'm sorry to get you out of an important meeting in London but you see I can't wait for six months. He's marrying my daughter tomorrow!

CAL: (PEERING ROUND DOOR.)
Daddy, do we have any gyroscopic agitators?

DA: (TO CAL)
Yeah, they're in the secret panel in the living room. (RETURNS TO TELEPHONE) Gerry c'mon so, you can't make an exception just this once?, one wee.... ...well thanks very much! (SLAMS RECEIVER DOWN)

PONDERS FOR A WHILE. WE SEE HIM MAKING A DECISION. HE DIALS A NEW NUMBER.

DA:
Hello, is that the INLA. I want to talk to you about this ceasefire. What, you accept this it are going along with it as well. ceasefire as well then! And that's the position of both of yis. Great.

THIS WON'T GET US INTO ONE OF THEIR FEUDS? WILL IT.

SLAMS RECEIVER DOWN

SCENE 30:   INT. UNCLE ANDY'S HOUSE. NIGHT.

THE TELEVISION NEWS IN ON IN B/G. UNCLE ANDY IS ON THE TELEPHONE

UNCLE ANDY:
Yes Blackie....so big Mervyn's going to do the driving, right,....He'll pick me up in half an hour, great. Yes it's Flat 47A Divis Tower....great.

(PUTS DOWN RECEIVER. RUBS HANDS. SITS DOWN AND WATCHES THE TELEVISION)

JULIAN STANDING BESIDE TOMBOLA, WITH A COUPLE OF KELLY AUDIENCE TYPES IN THE BACKGROUND

TV NEWSREADER:
Here, c'mere till I tell you about some of the the guests on Kelly tonight. From Coronation Street we've got Reg Holdsworth's sister, but first a wee bit news for you. The loyalist ceasefire comes into operation at midnight tonight. That's an end to all that nasty oul violence. And we'll bring you an updateon that fabulous news just as soon as we see whose won the tombola?....

(UNCLE ANDY BURIES HIS HEAD IN HIS HANDS. THEN GETS AN IDEA)

UNCLE ANDY:
Wait a minute, (LOOKS AT WATCH) it's twenty to twelve. I could get the bus...or a taxi...or...ah sod it, where's my morning suit.

WEDDING SCENE

NOTE: THIS IS ONE SET FOCUSING ON DIFFERENT SITUATIONS AT DIFFERENT
             PLACES AT THE WEDDING RECEPTION

SCENE 31: INT. LIVING ROOM. 47A DIVIS TOWER. NIGHT.

CAL SITS IN A DARKENED ROOM WITH A SINGLE LAMP. HE IS WORKING ON A DEVICE WITH A SOLDIERING IRON. HE IS READING INSTRUCTIONS FROM A BOOK -- "THE PRACTICAL TERRORIST - FOREWORD BY COLONEL GADAFFI". IT ALSO HAS A LARGE STICKER ON IT SAYING "REDUCED - HALF-PRICE". HE STOPS OCCASIONALLY AND CHUCKLES QUIETLY TO HIMSELF. THEN HE FLICKS THE SWITCH ON THE TIMING DEVICE TO TEST IT. IT MAKES A BUZZING SOUND AND RED LIGHT FLASHES.

CAL: (TRIUMPHANTLY)
Ha!   Ha!   Ha!   Ha!   The RUC band

are going to love this.

SCENE 32: INT. RECEPTION. DAY (DAY NINE)

WE OPEN WITH SHOT OF BILLY AND EMER AT RECEPTION. THERE IS A 6 PIECE JAZZ BAND DRESSED IN HAWAIIAN SHIRTS AND RUC HATS. DA AND UNCLE ANDY ARE SITTING TOGETHER.

BAND LEADER:
(HE SPEAKS WITH AN AFFECTED AMERICAN DRAWL).
Good afternoon ladies and gentlemen from the

Royal Ulster Constabulary. My name is Hugh and

this here is my band "The Interrogators" and

while we're around, you have absolutely no right

to silence. We're going to kick it off now - for all

of you true Blues lovers it's "The Green Grassy

Slopes of the Boyne. Ah 1, 2, 3,4.

THE BAND START PLAYING A MOVING VERSION OF THE GREEN GRASSY SLOPES OF THE BOYNE

DA:
Well Andy, who'd have thought a year ago that

we'd be sitting together at a wedding.

UNCLE ANDY:
Aye - changed times now. Time for compromise.

DA:
Yeah that's right....you Prods will have to

compromise and get used to a United Ireland.

UNCLE ANDY:
Well Seamus, I think the compromise is that

Ulster stays part of the UK forever and yous like

it or lump it.

(CAL WALKS PAST - THE HEAVY MUSIC FROM THE OPENING CREDITS BEGINS TO PLAY. WE FOLLOW CAL'S EYES AS HE LOOKS FROM HIS WATCH TO THE CAKE. HE HAS A KNOWING GRIN ON HIS FACE)

(THE BRITS ARRIVE AT THE BACK OF THE RECEPTION. PAUL AND MA SEE THEM)

PAUL:
What do yous want. I didn't do nothing! I'm

innocent.

OFFICER:
Nothing, it's just that we heard that there was a

serious party going on and we thought we'd

better come over and investigate it.

MA:
Come on in lads.

SOLDIER 1:
Get the lagers in Jeff......have you got any more

daughters?

DA:
Yes, that's right, Andy, we have to look to the

future and put the past behind us.

UNCLE ANDY:
Aye, we have to forgive and forget how you

started the Troubles in 1969 with your bombing

and shooting.

DA:
That's right - forgive and forget, how you started

it when you set up an Orange State in 1922.

Slainte.

UNCLE ANDY:
Cheers.

DA:
Slainte

UNCLE ANDY:
Cheers.

(SHOT OF CAL AS HE LOOKS AT HIS WATCH AND BACK TO THE CAKE. WE HEAR OFF CAMERA THE WORDS "PRAY SILENCE FOR THE BEST MAN")

Emer's in love, Ma's delighted and
Billy wonders if Da's going to pay for
the wedding. (No he's not.)

The wedding
party after the
fight

PAUL: **(STANDS TO MAKE SPEECH)**
We are here to celebrate the happy occasion of the wedding of Billy and Emer. Can I say I feel very happy today, almost as happy as the day I was released after serving 15 years in jail for a crime I did not commit. I don't think anyone can understand the mental anguish caused .....

DA:
You know Andy if there was more like you and me we wouldn't have had 25 years of troubles.

UNCLE ANDY:
That's right we could have stretched it out to 40.

(THEY BOTH LAUGH)

DA: (SEEING CAL PASSING)
Come and meet your new in law Cal, he's great *have a pint with your new in law* crack.

CAL: (HOLDING A REMOTE CONTROL DEVICE)
Stand at the back of the hall, Daddy. It's going to be a bit messy.

DA:
What?

UNCLE ANDY:
Here, Seamus, did you hear the one about Paisley becomin Catholic.....

(DADDY IS DISTRACTED FROM CAL AND LISTENS TO ANDY)

PAUL:
Then in the 13th year of my incarceration the Home Secretary belatedly referred my case back to the Court of Appeal cos the evidence, that was there from day 1, and was withheld from my defence lawyers, showed that I did not do it!

BILLY: (OUT OF SIDE OF MOUTH)
Could you wind it up please Paul.

UNCLE ANDY:
... and Paisley says to the nun, do mind if I call you Eileen. **(LAUGHS).**

DA: (LAUGHING)
Good one Andy!

CAL:
Not long now Daddy.

(WE SEE A SHOT OF THE CAKE. THE MUSIC BEGINS AGAIN)

PAUL:
So after finally winning my freedom granted

begrudgingly by the English Courts, I came home

to Belfast only to be put in jail by Billy here, for

something I did not do! So in conclusion I'd just

like to say "To the bride and groom!"

UNCLE ANDY:}   The bride and groom.
DA:}

(SHOT OF BILLY AND EMER MAKING THEIR WAY TO THE WEDDING CAKE)

CAL:
Any second now Daddy.

DA:
What do you mean Cal?

CAL:
Just watch the cake....it's my wedding surprise.

DA: (LOOKS   AT   CAL   THEN   CAKE
        REALISATION DAWNS)
Oh no not this Cal!

UNCLE ANDY:
What is it!

CAL:
Too late Daddy.

DA: (BURSTS THROUGH HIS TABLE AND RUNS TOWARDS CAKE IN SLOW MOTION)
No!   Get down.

BEFORE DA GETS TO THE CAKE CAL FLICKS SWITCH. CAKE DISSOLVES IN FLASH. C/A'S CUSTARD PIE SPLATS. SHOT OF CAKE TABLE STREWN WITH FRAGMENTS. TWO STICKS RISE UP AND PART - BANNER BETWEEN STICKS READS "UP THE REPUBLIC" WITH TRICOLOUR EITHER SIDE.   GREEN/WHITE/ORANGE FIREWORKS ALREADY LIT SURROUNDING HOLE. MEANTIME WE HEAR A RENDITION OF THE SOLDIERS SONG. CAL STANDS RIGIDLY TO ATTENTION. ALL THE OTHER CATHOLICS IN THE ROOM LEAP TO ATTENTION FOR THE ANTHEM.

BAND   LEADER: (IN A BROAD BELFAST ACCENT)
We're not standing for this. Right lads!

THE RUC BAND STRIKE UP A JAZZY VERSION OF GOD SAVE THE QUEEN. CATHOLICS SIT DOWN/STAND UP. ALL THE PROTESTANTS STAND TO ATTENTION. NEITHER ANTHEM CAN BE HEARD AMID THE CACOPHONY.

EMER:
It's all going wrong, Billy.

PAUL IS SHOUTING "I DIDN'T DO IT". DA HAS GOT UNCLE ANDY BY THE THROAT. UNCLE ANDY IS TRYING TO HIT DA WITH A BOTTLE. CAL IS FIGHTING WITH THE LEAD SINGER OF THE POLICE BAND. BILLY AND EMER MEET IN THE CENTRE OF THE DANCEFLOOR AMID THE CHAOS.

EMER:
I don't believe it, Billy.

BILLY:
Yeah, they're getting on a lot better than I

thought.

UNCLE ANDY STAGGERS PAST WITH A BOTTLE
IN HIS HAND.

UNCLE ANDY:
Great wedding, Billy! Welcome to the family,

love.

BILLY AND EMER KISS

MA:
Stop it! Yous should be ashamed of yourselves!

MA PRODUCED A BASEBALL BAT AND
LAUNCHES INTO THEN MIDDLE OF THE
FIGHTING CROWD.

MA:
Stop fighting. Stop fighting!

(SHE NOTICES THE CAMERA CREW) and you lot,

yous are as bad! *Do you think the community relations council will accept this as a proper credit for their grant?*

MA SWINGS THE BASEBALL BAT AT THE
CAMERA. THERE IS A BLACK OUT. THEN A
CAPTAION READS "THIS FILM WAS
SPONSORED BY THE COMMUNITY RELATIONS
COUNCIL". END TITLE SEQUENCE BEGINS WITH
THE MUSIC FROM THE CURRENT NIO ADVERT -
BEGINS "TURN, TURN, TURN" BY THE BYRDS.
WE SEE VARIOUS SCENES FROM THE FILM.
THE SEQUENCE FEATURES EACH CAST
MEMBER WITH ACCOMPANYING CAPTIONS.

SCENE 33: EXT. WEDDING RECEPTION. DAY.

NEW FINAL SCENE - CLOSE UP OF BILLY AND
EMER SITTING IN FRONT OF WHAT APPEARS
TO BE THE FRONT OF AN ORDINARY CAR.
BILLY AND EMER ARE IN THEIR WEDDING
GEAR. BILLY AND EMER LOOK LOVINGLY AT
EACH OTHER. BILLY STARTS TO DRIVE OFF.
CAMERA PULLS BACK TO REVEAL THAT THEY
ARE IN FACT SEATED IN THE FRONT OF A
POLICE LANDROVER. A LARGE BUMPER
STICKER ON THE WINDSCREEN READS "BILLY
AND EMER". THE LANDROVER IS BEDECKED
WITH RIBBONS ETC. THE LANDROVER DRIVES
PAST AND ON THE BACK OF THE LANDROVER
IS A PLACARD READING "JUST MARRIED."

END TITLES

billy

Origins

Billy can't remember his parents. As far as he can recall he always lived with his Uncle Andy. From the age of six Billy tried to look after Uncle Andy as best he could. But as anyone who has tried will tell you, raising a dyed-in-the-wool, bigoted Orange Elvis fan isn't easy. As a poor working-class Protestant kid who came through the worst years of the Troubles, Billy knew what he had to do; join the police and earn a bloody packet!

Fashion

Billy's work as a policeman dictates his fashion outlook. Whilst working he wears his smart police uniform set off by chicken tikka and burger relish stains, which were all acquired in the course of duty. The smell from these stains mingles with the odour of salt and vinegar to create an aroma that is unique to the RUC. Once you've smelt a cop's uniform you'll never forget it. For a long time Billy also adopted the classic RUC casual look – rugby shirt, jeans/chinos and slip-on moccasins (if you see any man wearing clothes like these, do not insult our boys in bottle green within his earshot). Dympna changed all that. In came V necks and cargoes but her efforts to make Billy cool have come to nowt as it is impossible to have street cred – except in the gay fraternity – whilst sporting a 'tache. Yet it is a rare sight for an RUC man to be seen without one. It is an incontrovertible fact that the majority of the RUC sport a moustache and the ratio is even higher for policewomen. The RUC cling to this facial fuzz because they believe it gives them a look of gravitas with the public. Unfortunately the public thinks it gives the police the look of the Village People circa 1978. The RUC – 93 per cent Protestant, 92 per cent moustached.

Hobbies

Policing contentious marches and collecting overtime, sitting in the back of a Land Rover eating pasties and copping off with Da's daughters.

billy

Q What is your favourite part of the day?

A Sleeping off last night's drink down the station.

Q What is your favourite book?

A My notebook.

Q No, I meant fiction.

A What I said, my notebook.

Q Whom do you prefer, Emer or Dympna?

A Dympna, definitely Dympna, though apparently Da has another daughter so I'd have to meet her to be absolutely sure.

Q Do you agree with a name change for the RUC?

A No, we've got quite used to being called 'black bastards'.

Q With a job like yours, have you ever been really scared?

A Yeah, Chris Patten really scares me at the minute.

Q Which living person do you most admire?

A Chris Patten. Remember I said that, Chris.

uncle andy

greasy slicked-down hair. His wardrobe is completed by his Elvis belt buckle that fulfils the dual function of demonstrating his undying loyalty to 'the king' and hiding his beer gut. If you wish to achieve 'the Uncle Andy look' we urge you to seek psychiatric help.

The mystery of Uncle Andy

Why Billy hasn't bucked him out of the house years ago . . .

Origins

Unknown. Is he really Billy's Uncle Andy or just his mother's 'particular friend'? The writers have yet to decide, so watch future episodes.

Politics

Middle of the road. Usually a Catholic one – with a sash on.

Fashion

Uncle Andy is a fashion icon. He single-handedly brought the string vest back into High Street stores. He has developed his own unique 'Protestant style', which includes a Viva Zapata moustache and Reactolite sunglasses – totally unnecessary in this climate but an essential loyalist fashion accessory since the seventies (also handy for hiding his lying eyes when he's pulling a fast one on Billy). His array of chunky jewellery adds a full stone to his weight and is only outshone by his

56

uncle andy

Q How do you start your day?

A As Ulster's sexiest man, I need my beauty sleep. But thanks to the Protestant work ethic, I'm usually up with the larks around twelveish.

Q What is your favourite part of the day?

A Happy hour in the Kneebreakers.

Q Which living person do you most admire?

A Elvis.

Q What's your favourite drink?

A One bought by somebody else.

Q If you could choose any job what would it be?

A Excuse me, do you work for the DSS? 'Cos if you do this interview's over.

Q What characteristic do you most dislike about yourself?

A I'm too tolerant of other people's views.

the long marching Season

Transmission date
16 January 1998

Let's be honest, when we wrote this script (summer 1997) the marching season wasn't quite as long as it is today. But it was long enough, so we thought that for the first episode of our brand-new comedy series we should address this serious issue.

It also seemed to be the perfect opportunity to reintroduce the characters from *Two Ceasefires and a Wedding* who made up the main cast. Like all first episodes, the plot was simple. Uncle Andy plans an Orange march somewhere it isn't wanted, Da and Cal object as concerned non-residents, Ma and Emer 'just want peace' and Billy is 'the pig in the middle'. The only problem was, where would be a suitable location for the march to pass through? Where better than the sleepy village of Ballykissangel for Uncle Andy to take to the Queen's highway and exercise his right to march (and his growing beer gut). We had already done a sketch on radio about an Orange march trailing a traditional route through Ballykissangel – it seemed like the perfect location.

So we all set off to the village of Avoca in County Wicklow, where Ballykissangel is filmed in real life. We painted the kerbstones red, white and blue and put up an Orange arch at the entrance to the village. We'd cleared it all with the locals beforehand and they all enjoyed it, especially the parish priest, for some reason! Some passing traffic hooted their horns as we marched. We were starting to get worried that we were seriously in danger of single-handedly saving the Orange Order's image. Then the *Daily Star* managed to find one 'concerned resident' who objected to what we were doing and splashed it in a full-colour spread in the paper's next edition. Suddenly we were making a controversial programme. And they say there'd be peace if it wasn't for the media?

damOn quinn

SCENE 1- MORNING

INT MA AND DA'S DARKENED BEDROOM. BOTH DA AND MA ARE LYING IN BED. THE CAMERA FOCUSES ON THE RADIO ALARM CLOCK. IT READS 10.59 IT THEN READS 11.00. A LOUD VOCIFEROUS RENDITION OF "MEN BEHIND THE WIRE" BLARES OUT. MA WAKES UP AND LOOKS OVER AT DA WHO CONTINUES TO SNORE.

THIS SCRIPT SEEMS LONG COULD WE CUT FIRST SCENE AND START AT SCENE 2? WE CAN ALWAYS USE MATERIAL AGAIN.

MA:
(GETTING UP AND SHOUTING)
GET UP!

DA DOES NOT MOVE SHE PULLS THE DUVET OFF DA TO REVEAL HIM FULLY CLOTHED. DRESSED IN A "REROUTE SECTARIAN MARCHES" T -SHIRT AND WITH A PLACARD CRADLED IN HIS ARM. MA ROLLS HER EYES. AGAIN SHOUTING

MA:
Get up!

DA CONTINUES TO SNORE

MA:
(LEANING IN TO DA'S EAR AND IN A STAGE WHISPER)
Hey there big man, how's about some hot sweaty loving?

DA:
(LEAPING UP STARTLED)
Woooah. Headache!

MA:
For an activist you're not very active.

DA:
Has the Orange march started?

MA:
Five minutes ago.

DA:
Typical Orange Order, not only do they trample over my rights, they do it at the skrake of dawn.

MA:
It's eleven o'clock.

DA:
It's still the bloody morning. There's no reason they couldn't have their march at two o'clock.

MA:
That's the Prods for you. Just full of badness.

(HE OPENS DOOR TO WALK INTO THE LIVING ROOM).

SCENE 2 – MORNING INT LIVING ROOM

DA:
Cal get up, you lazy scut, the march has started. Cal if you don't get up now you're going to miss being offended.

CAL:
I'm ready.

DA:
Aw come on Cal - you can't protest looking like that.

CAL:
This T-shirt is making an important political statement.

DA:
Barney?

CAL:
Aye - it's saying Orangemen are political dinosaurs.

DA:
Go and get your "Re-route the flute" T-shirt and stop your nonsense.

CAL:
I can't. Mammy put it in with the coloureds.

DA:
Come on we'll be late. Grab your placard.

DA AND CAL WALK OUT A LIVING ROOM DOOR.

SCENE 3 IMMEDIATELY LATER INT KITCHEN 47A DIVIS TOWER.

ENTER DA AND CAL. A TELESCOPE IS POSITIONED OUT THE WINDOW. DA TAKES THE TELESCOPE AND CAL LOOKS OUT THROUGH A PAIR OR BINOCULARS.

DA:
There it is. There's Larne.

CAL:
You got the road?

DA:
And there they are. It's a bit blurred but I can make out the Orange.

CAL:
(SHOUTING)
Re-route sectarian marches!

DA:
(SHOUTING)
Coat-trailing bastards.

MA:
(COMES IN)
And a very good morning to you too.

DA:
It is not a good morning. We the concerned residents of Divis Tower are being subjected to an outrageous display of sectarianism...

CAL:
(SHOUTING OUT THE WINDOW)
Orange scum!!!

MA:
And just 20 miles from your doorstep.
(SHAKING HEAD)
So what do you want for breakfast?

DA:
I'm on a diet, I'll just have a fry.

CAL:
Could you cut my toast up into soldiers?

DA: (Sharply)
What?

CAL:
Sorry Republican Freedom Fighters struggling against British oppression.

DA:
A look at that! There's the cops chatting away to them.
(PICKS UP A MEGAPHONE AND CHANTS) SS RUC!!! SS RUC!!!

MA:
I don't think they'll hear you in Larne.

DA:
That is not the point. The concerned residents have not given their consent. We tried to engage the Orange Order in dialogue. Cal even wrote them a letter.

CAL:
In my best Irish.

MA:
Why don't you just ignore the march?

DA:
(CONTEMPTUOUSLY)
Just ignore it! That's easy for you to say. It's not staring you in the face.
(PULLING MA OVER)
Just you take a look down that telescope and tell me to ignore it!

MA:

Oh for God's sake
(SHE LOOKS DOWN IT)
It's all blurred. Are you ever going to learn to focus this?
(SHE STARTS TO TWIDDLE THE LENS)

DA:

Croppys will not lie down.

MA:

Oh look there's a digger

CAL:

Daddy it's Drumcree four!

I WONDER IF THERE'LL BE A FIFTH OR SIXTH.

DA:

What a nauseauting triumphalist display. But then that's the Orange Order.

MA:

That's not the Orange Order.

DA:

What!

MA:

That's the DOE digging up the road.

DA:

What!! **(GRABS TELESCOPE OFF MA AND LOOKS DOWN IT) WE SEE THE SAID DOE WORKERS DRESSED IN ORANGE COATS DIGGING AT A**

ROAD.
(STANDS MOMENTARILY SILENCED. HE RECOVERS)
Those orange coats are offensive.

CAL: (PICKS UP MEGAPHONE)
SS DOE! SS DOE!

DA:

Shut up!

SCENE 4 - SAME DAY LATER
INT LIVING ROOM UNCLE ANDY'S HOUSE
ANDY (UNCLE ANDY IS LEANING OVER A PRAM DOTING ON HIS NEPHEW)

ARE WE GOING TO HAVE A BABY ON SET? BAD IDEA METHINKS

UNCLE ANDY:
Aw aren't you lovely. You're going to look great in this wee bowler hat and a sash.
(SHOWS THE HAT AND SASH TO BABY)
And next week I'll get you a wee plumed hat and a flutey. You'd like that wouldn't ye? Don't you worry son I'll make sure your Fenian ma doesn't indoctrinate you.

BILLY:
Oi Uncle Andy! I've told you before cut out the secrarian remarks about my wife.

UNCLE ANDY:
I'm not sectarian I just don't like Taigs. Never thought I'd see the day when I'd be living under the same roof as a papish. Why do you and your.... wife have to live here?

BILLY:
Cos it's my house and I pay the mortgage.

UNCLE ANDY:
I suppose that makes you think you own the place.

BILLY:
Emer's my wife. Will you please try and make her feel more at home.

UNCLE ANDY:
Okay, okay... I'll put some coal in the bath.

BILLY:
Oi!

UNCLE ANDY:
And I'll get a couple of pigs for the kitchen.

BILLY:
I've warned you!

UNCLE ANDY:
Aye you're right. One pig in the house is enough.

EMER:
(COMES DOWN THE STAIRS)
I better rush. Are you sure you'll be okay with my wee love?

UNCLE ANDY:
Don't you worry Carson Joel Craig will be safe with me.

EMER:
He's called Keanu that's what's on his birth certificate and that's the name we chose for him. Didn't we Billy?

BILLY:
Yes love you did. Now can we get going. I'll drop you off at your Ma's.

EMER:
Is it not out of your way?

BILLY:
Naw, it's no problem we're arresting the fella next door.

EMER:
Aw that's great. But I thought you were policing that Orange march in Knocknacloughy.

BILLY:
Naw that's not till this afternoon.

UNCLE ANDY:
Hold on a minute I'm babysitting so you and your Sinn Fein/IRA loving mates in the RUC can trample on the rights of the loyalist people to march through a 100% catholic town!

BILLY:
Uncle Andy the Chief Constable hasn't decided if the march will be allowed to go ahead or not. But if we speak to the Residents Committee...

UNCLE ANDY:
Residents Committee me arse! They're nothing but a bunch of fenians with no respect for the rule of law. I'm warning you Billy — if that march doesn't get through, we'll wreck the place.

SCENE 5 SAME DAY LATER EXT. KNOCKNACLOUGHY

AFTERNOON TIGHT SHOT OF BILLY AND ANOTHER RUC CONSTABLE STANDING AT A LANDROVER. A SENIOR RUC OFFICER IS ALSO THERE. IN THE BACKGROUND CAN BE HEARD AN ANGRY MOB AND ORANGE BAND MUSIC. BILLY AND THE OTHER CONSTABLE ARE DRESSED IN RIOT GEAR.

BILLY:
Well chief are we letting the Orange march through or not?

SENIOR OFFICER:
Well Billy it's not as simple as that. As the senior officer on the ground I have to consider all the relevant factors. The legitimate right to march as oppossed to the equally legitimate right to protest. The likelihood of a breach of the peace, the overall security situation and indeed the wider political implications of any decision I make.

THE CONSTABLES EXPRESS AWE AT THIS RESPONSIBILITY.

SENIOR OFFICER:
(PRODUCING COIN)
So heads it goes down. Tails we block it **(TOSSES A COIN)** – Tails.

BILLY:
(UNENTHUSIASTICALLY)
So we're blocking it?

SENIOR OFFICER:
(PAUSE)
Best of three?

FADE TO BLACK.

SCENE 6 SAME DAY LATER
EXT. KNOCKNACLOUGHY

AFTERNOON TIGHT SHOT OF BILLY AND ANOTHER RUC . CONSTABLE STANDING AT A LANDROVER. A SENIOR RUC OFFICER IS ALSO THERE. IN THE BACKGROUND CAN BE HEARD AN ANGRY MOB AND ORANGE BAND MUSIC. BILLY AND THE OTHER CONSTABLE ARE DRESSED IN RIOT GEAR. THE SENIOR OFFICER IS STILL TOSSING A COIN. THE CONSTABLES HAVE BEEN KEEPING SCORE.

SENIOR OFFICER:
(PLEASED).
Heads! What does that make it?

BILLY:
Eh 16 all.

SENIOR OFFICER:
Okay best of thirty three. Come on baby
(HE TOSSES COIN).
Yes heads. Yes!
(JUBILANTLY)
I have reluctantly decided that the march goes ahead.

SCENE 7 SAME DAY EVENING
INT UNCLE ANDY'S HOUSE LIVING
ROOM.

ANDY (OUR VIEW IS FROM THE CHILDS PERSPECTIVE IN THE PRAM. UNCLE ANDY'S FACE NEARLY FILLS THE WHOLE SCREEN. HE IS SERENADING KEANU USING THE RATTLE AS A MICROPHONE. BY THE SOUNDS OF IT THE CHILD IS DISTRESSED BY THIS SPECTACLE)

UNCLE ANDY:
Are you lonesome tonight?
Do you miss me tonight?
Are you sad that we drifted apart?
Does your memory stray....

THE CHILD IS NOW HYSTERICAL

UNCLE ANDY:
Alright. Alright. I'll play you a wee lullaby.

**(HE TURNS ON THE CD PLAYER. THE RAUCOUS STRAINS OF "THE GREEN GRASSY SLOPES OF THE BOYNE" BLARES OUT. UNCLE ANDY SINGS ALONG AND STARTS TO DANCE. HE TOSSES UP THE RATTLE IN THE MANNER OF A BANDLEADER AND CATCHES IT. THE KID SURPRISINGLY LIKES IT AND STARTS TO GURGLE. BILLY ENTERS DISHEVELLED AND EXHAUSTED.
BILLY SWITCHES OFF THE CD IN EXASPERATION.**

UNCLE ANDY:
(GENUINELY PLEASED)
Billy! You let the march through. That's my boy.
(PULLING HIS CHEEK AFFECTIONATELY)

BILLY:
It was a purely policing decision.

UNCLE ANDY:
So there was more of us than there was you.

BILLY:
Aye.

UNCLE ANDY:
Extra sausage in your fry tonight.
(HE HANDS BILLY A DRINK)
God bless the RUC impartially upholding the rule of law and sticking it to the fenians.

BILLY:
You saw the t.v. highlights then?

UNCLE ANDY:
Aye – you were great in that baton charge. Here what about tomorrows march through Ballyhacknacloy?

BILLY:
No decision's been made yet

UNCLE ANDY:
(JOCULARLY) No decisions been made yet. So when did yous not make the decision to let it through.

SCENE 8 NEXT DAY
EXT BALLYHACKNACLOY

AFTERNOON TIGHT SHOT OF BILLY AND ANOTHER RUC CONSTABLE STANIDNG AT A LANDROVER. A

SENIOR RUC OFFICER IS ALSO THERE. IN THE BACKGROUND CAN BE HEARD AN ANGRY MOB AND ORANGE BAND MUSIC. BILLY AND THE OTHER CONSTABLE ARE DRESSED IN RIOT GEAR.

BILLY
So are we letting the march down again?

SENIOR OFFICER:
No. After yesterdays march John Hume was furious. He got straight on to Dublin, they got Teddy Kennedy to phone Bill Clinton who rang Tony Blair who got on to Mo Mowlam. And they're all absolutely adamant. This time it has to be the best of three.

(PRODUCES COIN AND TOSSES).

SCENE 9 SAME DAY EVENING INT UNCLE ANDY'S HOUSE LIVING ROOM

UNCLE ANDY IS PULLING A GLASS OUT OF BILLY'S HAND. BILLY AGAIN LOOKS DISHEVELLED.

UNCLE ANDY:
Disgraceful! The loyalist people not allowed to march on their own Queens Highway. And when they try to have a dignified riot they are brutally batoned off the street by the Sinn Fein/IRA loving RUC.

BILLY:
Uncle Andy you can march in all the Protestant areas you want.

UNCLE ANDY:
Whats the point in that? An Orange march is no fun without fenians. You've pushed us so far against the wall we're over the brink of the abyss.

BILLY:
What?

UNCLE ANDY:
(PICKS UP PHONE AND DIALS)
If I didn't live here I'd put your windies in!

BILLY:
So it was you who painted "SS RUC" on the side of the house.

UNCLE ANDY:
The loyalist people are angry

BILLY:
I wouldn't mind but you spelt it wrong.
A BIT RICH COMING FROM ME!

UNCLE ANDY:
(TO PHONE)
Mervyn, emergency meeting my house now.

BILLY:
That's it I'm going to the in-laws. At least they'll be pleased to see me today.

UNCLE ANDY:
(PUTTING DOWN PHONE)
I'm telling you Billy the police are finished in this area. Finished!

BILLY:
See you later Uncle Andy.

UNCLE ANDY:
(HURT)
You not going to give me a lift round to the offy

BILLY:
Alright.

UNCLE ANDY:
And here - lend us a tenner would you?

SCENE 10 SAME DAY EVENING
INT LIVING ROOM 47A DIVIS TOWER

BILLY, EMER, MA, DA, AND CAL ARE
ALL IN THE ROOM. DA IS COO-ING OVER THE BABY WHICH IS IN A PRAM.

DA:
Aww how is Plunket Donnacha Kevin Barry?

EMER:
His name is Keanu.

CAL:
Well its a very silly name.

BILLY:
So Da, did you see me on TV today? Protecting the nationalist community of Ballyhacknacloy from the loyalist mobs?

MA:
Och that was awful nice of Billy. I said to the woman in the laundry. "See that peeler dragging that fella by the hair and throwing him into the back of the landrover? That's my son in law."

EMER:
Are you not going to thank Billy? Like he went out of his way to please you. He fired plastic bullets at the Orangemen and everything.

DA:
Oh so I now have to thank the RUC for not living in fear for a day.

MA:
Fear. The only thing you're afraid of is a job.

DA:
I have to thank you cos the RUC reroute one orange march.

CAL:
Yes if you keep rerouting them the concerned residents will have nothing to be concerned about. Then where would we be?

SHOULD DA REACT HERE?

MA:
Well if you're so concerned why didn't you go down to Ballyhacknacloy yourself.

DA:
If I'd gone there would have been violence.

EMER:
From the loyalists?

DA:
No from the residents committee. That's Cuivan O'Muilliaths patch. He'd go buck mad if we tried to steal his limelight.

CAL:
Is Cuivan not Knocknacloughy?

DA:
No thats Gaeroid O'Riorgeneath.

CAL:
Is he not Cloughadoyee?

DA:
No that's Cecil Fortiscue.

LOVE THIS. IT'LL GET NO LAUGHS.

CAL:
I wouldn't mind but none of them can string two words together.

DA:
Did you see Cuivan on the news with Rose Neill? She wiped the floor with him.

CAL:
It's not fair. We'll never get to be a proper concerned residents group. The Orange Order just refuse to march up the Falls Road.

MA:
Well why don't you invite them to?

DA:
Don't be stupid how can you invite someone you object to.

SCENE 11 – SAME NIGHT
INT KITCHEN 47A DIVIS TOWER.

CAL IS ON THE PHONE. HE IS HOLDING A LARGE HISTORY BOOK

CAL:
Hello is that the Orange Order. Can I speak to the Grand Wizard....Grand Master yes he'll do. Hello, I was wondering have you ever considered having an Orange March up the Falls Road? Yes it is traditional actually, because if you read up on it there was one in l872. Caused a pitch battle....lasted for days. Of course I'm an Orangeman!   What lodge am I from? Well originally Turf and then the New Lodge.

THE LINE HAS GONE DEAD
CAL REACTS

SCENE 12 SAME NIGHT
INT UNCLE ANDY'S HOUSE

UNCLE ANDY AND MERVYN ARE SITTING AT THE TABLE. THEY HAVE A MAP. THEY ARE DRINKING BEER.

UNCLE ANDY:
The loyalist people have been betrayed by the British Government, the RUC, the Unionist Parties, the loyal institutions.

BIG MERVYN:
So the loyalist people have been betrayed by the loyalist people.

UNCLE ANDY:
Exactly Mervyn, which is why we must re-establish our civil and religious liberties by stirring it up bad somewhere.

BIG MERVYN:
Another march?

UNCLE ANDY:
An excellent idea Mervyn. Right here's a map, heres a pin, close your eyes and pick us somewhere to march that's hiving with fenians.

MERVYN DOES AS INSTRUCTED

UNCLE ANDY:
Crossmaglen? Eh no Mervyn. The British army can't even march through there.

MERVYN GOES THROUGH THE PROCESS AGAIN

UNCLE ANDY:
The Irish Sea...Naw only Big Ian walks on water.

MERVYN GOES THROUGH THE PROCESS AGAIN

UNCLE ANDY:
That is genius Mervyn
MERVYN OPENS HIS EYES

UNCLE ANDY:
Aw that is beautiful if we can put an Orange march through there we can cause more chaos and bad feeling than Cabletel.

DA:
No we won't – because our day has come Cal and I are now Chair and Vice Chair of the Concerned Residents of Ballykissangel.

MA:
Do the residents of Ballykissangel know this?

DA:
Eh...not yet.

MA:
They'll be even more concerned when they do!

SCENE 12A - INT. LIVING ROOM 47A DIVIS TOWER

CAL AND MA ARE THERE. DA BURSTS INTO THE ROOM WITH A PAPER.

DA:
Ballykissangel! Cal, the Orange Order are going to march through Ballykissangel!

MA:
You'll need the Hubble Telescope to see that.

SCENE 13

A SERIES OF FLASHED UP NEWSPAPER HEADLINES FX - THROUGHOUT THIS SEQUENCE THE THEME FROM BALLYKISSANGEL IS PLAYING BIG PICTURE OF UNCLE ANDY HEADLINE READS "I WILL MARCH IN BALLY K" NEWSLETTER BIG PICTURE OF CAL AND DA. THE HEADLINE READS "OH NO YOU WON'T" IRISH NEWS BIG PICTURE OF UNCLE ANDY THE HEADLINE READS "OH YES I WILL"

NEWSLETTER BIG PICTURE OF CAL AND DA. THE HEADLINE READS "YOU AND WHOSE ARMY?" IRISH NEWS.

SCENE 14

A FEW DAYS LATER DAYTIME INT A CAR.
BIG MERVYN IS DRIVING AND UNCLE ANDY IS IN THE PASSENGER SEAT.

UNCLE ANDY:
Right this is the frontier. Don't panic. You've had all your innoculations.

BIG MERVYN:
(RUBBING HIS ARM IN SELF PITY)
Typhoid near killed me.

UNCLE ANDY:
You've got your passport. Now remember if you're are captured by the enemy, just give them your name, rank and lodge number. Right! Take us up to check point Paddy.

SCENE 15 SAME DAY
EXT. AT THE BORDER.

UNCLE ANDY'S CAR PASSES BY A SOUTHERN CUSTOMS OFFICER WHO LAZILY WAVES THEM ON. THE CAR DRIVES ON WE HEAR UNCLE ANDY'S VOICE

UNCLE ANDY:
Aw that is ridiculous. Mervyn stop the car.

THE CAR SCREECHES TO A HALT AND REVERSES TO THE CUSTOMS HUT ANDY AND MERVYN STEP OUT OF THE CAR AND WAVE THEIR PASSPORTS AT THE OFFICIAL.

UNCLE ANDY:
Uncle Andy here. British citizen. Do you speak English?

OFFICIAL:
How are you.

UNCLE ANDY:
As a citizen of Great Britain and Ulster I wish to complain about your failure to stop and search this car. No doubt you thought that me and big Mervyn were members of the IRA.

THIS WOULD BE EVEN FUNNIER IF THEY ARE WEARING SASHES.

OFFICIAL:
No, I just thought you looked harmless.

UNCLE ANDY:
Well I insist that you search this vehicle or I shall have no option but to complain to the nearest British embassy about the appalling lack of security along the frontier with the United Kingdom.

OFFICIAL:
(NOT MOVING FROM HIS SPOT)
Okay if you insist.

(HE LEANS OVER AND GIVES THE CAR A CURSORY GLANCE).

That looks fine. On yis go.

THEY GET INTO THE CAR

UNCLE ANDY:
See what I mean. We've hardly crossed the border and we're being harrassed. It's a fenian police state that's what it is. Not safe for Protestants.

THE OFFICIAL WAVES THEM ON HE THEN TURNS AND WALKS INTO THE HUT.

SCENE 16 - IMMEDIATELY LATER SAME DAY - EXT. AT THE BORDER OTHER SIDE OF THE CUSTOMS HUT.

THE OFFICIAL STEPS OUT. THE CAMERA PULLS BACK TO REVEAL CAL AND DA WITH THEIR WHITE HIACE VAN BEING SEARCHED. CAL AND DA ARE DRESSED ONLY IN UNDERPANTS. THEY ARE SURROUNDED BY HEAVILY ARMED IRISH ARMY TROOPS.

DA:
No need to apologise captain the strip search was no trouble at all. The three hours just flew by.

CAL:
Go raibh maith agaith

SCENE 17 IMMEDIATELY LATER SAME DAY – EXT AT THE BORDER.

WE SEE A RUC LANDROVER SPEED PAST THE CUSTOMS HUT. THE OFFICIAL WAVES IT THROUGH ...THEN DOUBLE TAKES.

OFFICIAL:
I think that fellas lost.

SCENE 18 IMMEDIATELY LATER
SAME DAY – INT. RUC LANDROVER

BILLY, MA AND EMER. MA & EMER ARE DRESSED IN HIPPY PEACE TYPE GEAR. MA AND EMER ARE SINGING. THEY HAVE A TAMBOURINE AND GUITAR.

MA/EMER:
All we are saying is give peace a chance
All we are saying is give peace a chance
All we are saying is give peace a chance.

BILLY: (CRACKING UP)
Will you give my ears a chance!

MA:
We have to sing Billy - it's what you do at a peace camp.

BILLY:
But does it have to be that song over and over again?

EMER:
It does actually. It's one of the approved songs in Peace for Beginners

(PRODUCES BOOKLET "PEACE FOR BEGINNERS")

MA:
Emer, have we got everything?

EMER:
I think so. Candles for the vigil?

MA PRODUCES TWO CANDLES FROM A BOX

MA:
Yes

EMER:
Cardboard doves?

MA PRODUCES TWO WHITE CARDBOARD DOVES

EMER:
Wee girls poem?

MA:
Wee girls poem?

EMER:
You have to have the badly written poem by the six year old about the suffering, alls I know is violence and when is it going to end.

MA:
I'll do it myself. Have you got any crayons?

VERY CYNICAL, GUYS!

EMER:
(SINGING)
Alls we are saying is give peace.....

BILLY:
No, no, please! Can we not just listen to the radio for a while.

EMER:
Alright, alright.
BILLY SWITCHES ON THE RADIO

VOICE OVER
ALLS WE ARE SAYING IS GIVE PEACE A CHANCE

BILLY REACTS

SCENE 18A - INT. WHITE HIACE VAN

DA & CAL

CAL:
So daddy we turn left here at Ballynaskelliga, six miles on we turn right for Scraiginnamaffy and then there's a short cut over the Creevenablahy mountains to Ballykissangel.

DA:
There's no chance of Uncle Andy getting there before us.

CAL:
Especially as we've nicked all these

(WE SEE THE BACK OF THE VAN WITH LOTS OF ROAD SIGNS. NEWRY, DUBLIN ETC.)

DA:
Not that we need road signs Cal, because we Gaels intuitively have an intimate knowledge of our native land.

CAL:
The RAC road map helps as well.

CAL PRODUCES MAP

DA:
Cal the true Gael does not need maps.

CAL:
You're right daddy.

CAL THROWS MAP OUT THE WINDOW

SCENE 18B - EXT.

THE WHITE HIACE HAS STOPPED, CAL IS LOOKING AT SOME ROAD SIGNS

DA:
(SCREAMING)
Where the hell are we!

CAL:
(LOOKING AT SIGNS FROM THE BACK OF THE VAN)
Well we turned right at Rossaking in Kerry. Or was it left? No it was right. Then we went through Muckinasloe...four times
(TOSSING ASIDE SIGN)
So I reckon we should ask someone.

(DA HAS A LARGE POLE WITH SIGNS ON IT - HE SWINGS IT AT CAL)

SCENE 18C – EXT.

RUC LANDROVER IS TRAVELLING ALONG A COUNTRY ROAD. WE HEAR MA AND EMER SINGING OUT OF TUNE "CUM BYE YA" AND PLAYING GUITAR AND TAMBOURINE. THE LANDROVER SCREECHES TO A HALT. BILLY'S DOOR OPENS. THE GUITAR IS SLUNG UNCEREMONIOUSLY OUT OF THE LANDROVER. THERE IS A PAUSE. BILLY THEN THROWS OUT THE TAMBOURINE. BILLY STARTS THE LANDROVER. WE THEN HEAR

THE SOUND OF MA AND EMER PLAYING "CUM BYE YA" ON THE SPOONS AND MOUTHORGAN. WE SEE THROUGH THE WINDSCREEN MA IS PLAYING THE MOUTHORGAN AND EMER THE SPOONS. BILLY REACTS.

SCENE 18D - EXT WHITE HIACE VAN IT IS STATIONARY

DA IS AT THE BONNET TRYING TO FIX THE VAN WHICH HAS OBVIOUSLY BROKEN DOWN. CAL LOOKS ON.

DA:
(LOOKING KNOWLEDGABLE)
Ah, I see what's wrong here yes. Just give me the spanner there....

CAL PASSES HIM THE SPANNER

DA:
And a drop of oil....

CAL PASSES DA THE OIL

DA:
The monkey wrench......

SCENE FADES OUT. FADES UP.

DA:

Just get us the hammer there.

CAL GOES TO THE TOOLBOX AND GETS THE HAMMER HE PASSES IT TO DA. DA SETS ABOUT THE ENGINE WITH THE LARGE HAMMER.

DA:

You stupid bloody machine.
Start! Start!

CAL PULLS DA AWAY. DA STILL TRIES TO ATTACK THE ENGINE SWINGING HIS BOOTS AT IT.

CAL:

Daddy it's alright there's somebody coming we'll hitch a lift.

CAL RUNS DOWN TO THE SIDE OF THE ROAD AND STICKS HIS THUMB OUT. UNCLE ANDY'S CAR ROARS PAST. WE SEE CAL BEING STRUCK ON THE HEAD AND BEING KNOCKED OUT BY A BEER CAN. THE CAR PASSES DA. UNCLE ANDY AND BIG MERVYN MAKE RUDE GESTURES TO DA AS THEY PASS.

SCENE 18E –

THE SCREEN IS COMPLETELY BLACK. WE HEAR SOUNDS OF THE NIGHT AND THE FOOTSTEPS OF TWO PEOPLE WALKING. WE HEAR THE VOICE OF CAL.

CAL:

Daddy it's pitch black. Do you think we're nearly there?

DA:

How the hell would I know I can't see in front of me. For all I know we could have been there already.

CAL:

Ah well look on the brightside.....

CAL AND DA LET OUT A SCREAM WHICH FADES. AS THEY FALL, WE HEAR THEM LAND IN WATER.

DA:

Swim, Cal swim!

CAL:

Where to.....?

VERY SILLY COULD WE CUT IT AND KEEP IT FOR LATER?

give my head peace

Da and Cal regret not joining the RAC for political reasons

SCENE 19 DAY

EXT AERIAL SHOT OF
BALLYKISSANGEL – THE TITLE
SEQUENCE FOOTAGE WOULD BE
PERFECT. THE BALLYKISSANGEL
THEME PLAYS.

SCENE 20A – THE BRIDGE AT BALLYKISSANGEL

THE BALLYKISSANGEL THEME
CONTINUES UNCLE ANDY AND BIG
MERVYN ARE STRUTTING ABOUT
DECKED OUT IN THEIR ORANGE
FINERY.

SCENE 20B – THE BRIDGE AT BALLYKISSANGEL

THE BALLYKISSANGEL THEME
CONTINUES CAMERA PULLS BACK
TO REVEAL MERVYN APPLYING THE
FINISHING TOUCHES TO HIS
ARTWORK. HE HAS PAINTED THE
KERBSTONES AT ONE END OF THE
BRIDGE RED, WHITE AND BLUE.
ANDY NODS APPROVINGLY.

SCENE 20C - THE BRIDGE AT BALLYKISSANGEL

THE BALLYKISSANGEL THEME
CONTINUES. ANDY IS STRUTTING
ABOUT WITH A CEREMONIAL
ROD. HE TOSSES IT INTO THE AIR.
HE AND MERVYN LOOK UP,
REALISE IT'S GOING TO FALL
ON TOP OF THEM, AND SCATTER
AWAY. THE ROD FALLS TO
THE GROUND.

SCENE 21 – THE BRIDGE AT BALLYKISSANGEL

UNCLE ANDY AND BIG MERVYN
MARCH UP TO EACH OTHER IN
MILITARISTIC FASHION. THEY TURN
ABOUT FACING THE TOWN AND
ARE ABOUT TO START THEIR
MARCH.

UNCLE ANDY:
Right Mervyn it's time to share our
culture and heritage with the people
of Eire....oh what have we here?

WE SEE THE GARDA APPROACHING
ACROSS THE BRIDGE.

Before the cameras roll – Cal practises being hit with a beer can

. . . it took twenty takes but we all enjoyed it!

UNCLE ANDY:
....a storm trooper of the hostile foreign state.

THE GARDA WALKS UP TO UNCLE ANDY AND BIG MERVYN.

GARDA:
Morning fellas. Very nice, very colourful.

UNCLE ANDY:
Don't you be taking the Mick. I suppose you've come to tell us we're not allowed to march on our own Queens highway.

BIG MERVYN:
As was

UNCLE ANDY:
Well we will not be dictated to by the pan Nationalist Front.

BIG MERVYN:
The Loyalist people have a right to march and we are gonna march right now.

GARDA:
Great.

UNCLE ANDY/MERVYN:
What?

GARDA:
I was just coming to say why don't you have it now.

UNCLE ANDY:
Now?

GARDA:
Fine, yeah, c'mon

MERVYN GOES TO MARCH. UNCLE ANDY PULLS HIM BACK.

UNCLE ANDY:
Hould on a minute Mervyn.

HE TURNS TO THE GARDA AND FOLDS HIS ARMS

UNCLE ANDY:
The Loyalist people will not be told they can march whenever, wherever they want by some stooge of the dirty Dublin dictat.

BIG MERVYN:
You tell him Andy.

GARDA:
OK don't march.

UNCLE ANDY:
Oh, don't march. Now the mask slips! The hidden agenda emerges Mervyn. This is a trojan horse in sheeps clothing

GARDA:
Fellas, I'm lost.

BIG MERVYN:
So am I Andy, are we marching or not?

WE HEAR DA'S VOICE SHOUTING

DA:
You're not marching here!

WE SEE DA AND CAL ARRIVING ON BIKES AT THE OTHER END OF THE BRIDGE.

CAL:
Re-route sectarian marches!

DA CAN'T STOP HIS BIKE.

DA:
Cal, what's wrong with these brakes?

DA'S BIKE FLIES PAST. WE HEAR A CRASH OFF CAMERA.

SCENE 22 – EXT THE BRIDGE AT BALLYKISSANGEL

THE STAND OFF HAS DEVELOPED. DA AND CAL FACE UNCLE ANDY AND MERVYN AT OPPOSITE ENDS OF THE BRIDGE. THE KERB STONES AT DA AND CAL'S END ARE NOW PAINTED GREEN, WHITE AND ORANGE. DA AND CAL HAVE PLACARDS WITH "NO TALK, NO WALK" AND "RE-ROUTE THE FLUTE". DA'S ARM IS IN A SLING. UNCLE ANDY AND MERVYN HAVE PLACARDS WITH "WALK DON'T TALK" AND "NO POPERY HERE". IN THE MIDDLE OF THE BRIDGE THE GARDA SITS ON A CRATE DRINKING TEA FROM A FLASK. HE IS CLEARLY BORED.

**SCENE 23 –
EXT BALLYKISSANGEL**

CHET GUPPY AMERICAN NEWS REPORTER STANDS AT THE VILLAGE SIGN FOR BALLYKISSANGEL PRESENTING HIS REPORT. THE FILM QUALITY IS EXACTLY AS PER C.N.N. THE C.R.A.P. LOGO IS AT THE BOTTOM RIGHT HAND CORNER.

CHET GUPPY:
The Ballykissangel stand off is now in it's tenth hour. With no sign of a breakthrough it seems only a matter of time before violence erupts. And we're expecting that anytime now...
(SHIFTY PAUSE.)
No. No violence yet. Sorry about that but we're hoping to bring you some disturbing images in time for the three o'clock bulletin.

SCENE 24 DAY
EXT BALLYKISSANGEL

AN ITALIAN FEMALE REPORTER GESTICULATING MADLY WITH OVER THE TOP MAKE UP AND JEWELLERY STANDS AT THE VILLAGE SIGN FOR BALLYKISSANGEL PRESENTING HER REPORT. THE FILM QUALITY IS STILL POOR ITALIAN LOGO IS AT THE BOTTOM RIGHT HAND CORNER. SHE JABBERS IN ITALIAN. INTERSPERSED WITH THE WORDS "DA", "CAL" "UNCLE ANDY" "GRANDE MERVYN" "MUSSOLINI" "FASCISTI" "ROUTA TRADITIONALE"

GREAT DIALOGUE!

SCENE 25 DAY
EXT BALLYKISSANGEL -

A SWEDISH REPORTER STANDS AT EXACTLY THE SAME SPOT THE SWEDISH LOGO IS AT THE BOTTOM RIGHT HAND CORNER. THE NAME LARS OLSEN IS CAPTIONED. BEING SO TALL THE CAMERA IS FILMING HIM A MIDRIFF SO HE HAS TO BEND DOWN TO GET HIS FACE INTO THE CAMERA. HE TALKS IN SWEDISH. THE REPORT IS INTERSPERSED WITH THE WORDS. "BALLYKISSANGEL" "ORANGE FEET" "FATHER CLIFFORD" HE LAUGHS AS IF HE'S MADE A JOKE.

THIS JOKE IS JUST TOO WILK!

SCENE 26 DAY
EXT BALLYKISSANGEL.

A JAPANESE REPORTER IS STANDING ON EXACTLY THE SAME SPOT. THERE IS JAPANESE WRITING UP THE SIDE OF THE PICTURE. HE SPEAKS IN JAPANESE INTERSPERSED WITH THE WORDS "UNCLE ANDY" "BIG MERVYN" "DA AND CAL" "STAND OFF" CULMINATING IN HIM SHOUTING "MURPHYS!"

THIS SHOULD KEEP US IN WITH THE RACE RELATIONS BOYS!

SCENE 27 DAY – EXT BALLYKISSANGEL.

CHET GUPPY AMERICAN NEWS REPORTER STANDS AT THE VILLAGE SIGN FOR BALLYKISSANGEL PRESENTING HIS REPORT. THE FILM QUALITY IS EXACTLY AS PER C.N.N. THE C.R.A.P. LOGO IS AT THE BOTTOM RIGHT HAND CORNER.

CHET GUPPY:
Hi I'm Chet Guppy. We're still waiting for the violence here. We're hoping to bring you that about five o'clock. Earlier I spoke to the leader of the Orangemen Uncle Andy. I asked him why the Orangemen want to march through Ballykissangel.

SCENE 28 DAY EXT BALLYKISSANGEL.

UNCLE ANDY AND BIG MERVYN ARE STANDING ON THE BRIDGE.

UNCLE ANDY:
Well it's traditional

CHET GUPPY:
(OFF CAMERA)
But you've never marched through Ballykissangel.

UNCLE ANDY:
(AGGRESSIVELY)
Aye but if we march this year it'll be traditional next year. And the next year, and the next year.

BIG MERVYN:
See how it works?

SCENE 29 DAY - EXT BALLYKISSANGEL.

DA AND CAL ARE STANDING. (PRE-RECORD CHET'S QUESTIONS)

CHET GUPPY: (VOICE OVER)
The Residents Committee take a different view.

DA:
There is a principle of consent here. And the Orangemen have not even asked us for our consent.

CHET GUPPY:
(OFF CAMERA)
And if they did ask you what
would you say?

CAL:
Piss off you're not marching here.

DA LOOKS ASKANCE

GREAT!

SCENE 30 DAY
EXT BALLYKISSANGEL.

MA IS SHOT CLOSE UP ON CAMERA.

CHET GUPPY:
(VOICE OVER)
If however there is to be no violence
(TURNING SLIGHTLY BITTER) it'll
be thanks to the dogooders who
took it on themselves to set up the
Ballykissangel Peace camp.

MA:
Well we felt very strongly that somebody
had to come down here and make a
stand for peace. We are sick to death
of marches, Orange marches,
Nationalist marches, it doesn't matter.
We're sick of marches.

CHET GUPPY:
(VOICE OVER)
So what are your plans?
MA: TO MARCH..FOR PEACE!
We're going to have a peace march.
                    ↑
                 BETTER GAG.

CHET GUPPY:
You seem pretty determined.

MA:
We're prepared to sit out here and
endure any hardship, any deprivation,
for the cause of peace.

THE CAMERA PULLS OUT TO
REVEAL EMER LYING IN A
SWIMSUIT ON A SUN LOUNGER
WITH SUNGLASSES. BILLY
STANDING OVER A BARBEQUE
DRESSED IN A HAWAIN SHIRT. A
SWING BALL AND A TENT ARE IN
THE BACKGROUND

BILLY:
Chicken wing Ma?

CHET GUPPY:
This stand off could last weeks. How
long are you going to stay here?

MA:
We intend to stay here... for two days if
the weather holds. And then we're
going to go down to Killarney to do the

ring of Kerry and Billy wants to see the book of Kells on the way back.

EMER:
Och Billy, you've burnt the burgers!

BILLY:
Aye well if you'd of watched them instead of lying about on your arse like lady muck!

AN ARGUMENT ENSUES

CHET GUPPY:
Well, good luck with your peace camp.

SCENE 31 DAY
EXT BALLYKISSANGEL.

DA, CAL, UNCLE ANDY, BIG MERVYN AND THE GARDA ARE STANDING ON THE BRIDGE THE STAND OFF IS CONTINUING. THE GUARD CALLS THE TWO SIDES OVER

GARDA:
Right lads I've some faxes here for you. "Stop the madness" – that's from Bill Clinton... "Keep up the madness" Ian

Paisley. Oh and Mervyn one from your mammy. "Did you get Father Clifford's autograph?"

BIG MERVYN:
Aye I did.....

TAKES OUT AUTOGRAPH BOOK. UNCLE ANDY LOOKS AT MERVYN ACCUSINGLY

BIG MERVYN:
Sorry Uncle Andy.

GARDA:
Fellas you've been here all day, could we not sort this out in the pub?

UNCLE ANDY:
No

DA:
No way

GARDA:
You don't mind if I go do you?

DA:
Not at all.

GARDA:
Well listen fellas, if you do decide to have a riot, give us a shout - I'll be in Fitzgeralds.

SCENE 32 DAY LATER
EXT BALLYKISSANGEL.

DA, CAL, UNCLE ANDY, BIG MERVYN
ARE CONTINUING THEIR STAND
OFF. SPAGHETTI WESTERN MUSIC
CUTS IN. WE HAVE A SEQUENCE
OF CLOSE UP SHOTS OF THEIR
FACES AND EYES A LA SERGIO
LEONE. THE SHOTS BETWEEN THE
FACES GET FASTER AND FASTER
TO A RIDICULOUS LEVEL CAMERA
SETTLES ON CALS FACE.

CAL:
Daddy?

Love this but it doesn't add much to plot - should we cut it.

DA:
Yes Cal

CAL:
Can I go to the toily.
(HE SCURRIES OFF)

SCENE 32A –
EXT. FITZGERALDS PUB

BILLY AND THE GARDA ARE
TALKING, SUPPING PINTS OUTSIDE
FITZGERALDS.

GARDA:
God this is wild exciting

BILLY:
So Felim are you going to let them
march or not?

GARDA:
No Billy I thought I'd just leave them
alone they'll get bored.

BILLY:
No we tried that it doesn't work

GARDA:
So how would the RUC handle this?

BILLY:
Oh we'd probably just cancel all leave,
swamp the area with police, fly in a
couple of crack army units, helicopter
support, throw up a razor wire corden,
put the population under house arrest,
baton protesters off the street, force the
march through, create a public relations
nightmare and generate a legacy of
distrust and bad feeling which should
last into the next millennium.

Suppose I have to say this at speed?

GARDA:
Softly, softly then...you know I don't
think we even have a helicopter.

BILLY:
No mate, you want to leather in there, beat all round you, crack a few scones...that's what policing is all about.

GARDA:
I've got a notebook I suppose I could threaten to take their names.

BILLY:
Do you want a lend of my plastic bullet gun.

GARDA:
Och no,

BILLY:
Go on, go on

GARDA:
No, no, ... could I?

BILLY:
I tell you what we'll get another couple of pints and I'll show you how it works.

SCENE 33 NIGHT TIME LATER EXT BALLYKISSANGEL.

IT IS DARK. DA, CAL, UNCLE ANDY AND BIG MERVYN ARE CLEARLY MISERABLE.

BIG MERVYN:
I'm starving Uncle Andy.

UNCLE ANDY:
Never mind.

BIG MERVYN:
But I haven't eaten for hours. It's worse than a loyalist hungerstrike.

UNCLE ANDY:
Alright don't go on.

BIG MERVYN:
At the Drumcree stand off there was chip vans. You could get burgers, pasties, jumbo hot dogs with relish, mustard anything you wanted like........

SCENE 34 – EXT BALLYKISSANGEL.

T IS DARK. DA, CAL, UNCLE ANDY AND BIG MERVYN ARE CLEARLY STILL MISERABLE. CAL AND DA LOOK VERY HUNGRY. WE CAN HEAR THEIR STOMACHS RUMBLING. BILLY, MA, AND EMER WALK BY CHEERILY.

BILLY:
I am stuffed. That steak was like half a cow!

EMER:
I couldn't look at another scampi.

MA:
Here I thought the free state bars
stayed open all night.

EMER:
It would have done only for that wee
Garda turning up with a plastic bullet
gun. Where'd he get that?

BILLY:
Anyway girls there's plenty of
drink in the tent.

DA AND CAL LOOK ON MISERABLY

CAL:
I'm cold daddy.

DA:
I told you to bring a coat.

CAL:
It was hot before. Now it's freezing.

DA:
At least it's dry.

**FX RAIN CUTS IN IMMEDIATELY ALL
FOUR PROTAGONISTS LOOK UP AT
THE SKY**

DA:
Well ....ish!

**SCENE 35 NIGHT TIME LATER
EXT BALLYKISSANGEL.**

**IT IS DARK. DA, CAL, UNCLE ANDY
AND BIG MERVYN ARE CLEARLY
STILL MISERABLE AND ARE
NOW BEING SOAKED.**

I'M LOOKING FORWARD TO THIS.

BIG MERVYN:
...They'd soup, there was stew. And
one wee van did a lovely fish. There
was cod or haddock you had a choice.

UNCLE ANDY:
**(PULLING OUT A MOBILE PHONE
AND DIALLING IT)**
Alright will you shut up! Hello Da?

DA:
(ANSWERING PHONE)
Hello – Concerned Residents of
Ballykissangel. Chair speaking.

UNCLE ANDY:
Now I want to make it clear that I am
not negotiating with Sinn Fein/IRA about
anything to do with our right
to march. But on the grounds that
it's pissing down can I suggest

that we continue our stand off in a neutral and dry venue?

DA:
Where would you suggest?

UNCLE ANDY:
The back of our Billy's landrover.

DA:
Well I will take that proposal and bring it to the Committee of Ballykissangel Concerned Residents and I will get back to you in due course.
(TO CAL)
Do you want to get dried off?

CAL NODS MISERABLY

DA:
You're on Andy. Come on for God's sake.
THEY ALL SCURRY OFF

SCENE 36 – EXT BALLYKISSANGEL

**LANDROVER IN RAIN
VOICE OVER**

MERVYN:
Then there was a pizza delivery van. They could do you deep pan, thin crust, calzone, the heap.

UNCLE ANDY:
Will you belt up Mervyn

CAL:
This is the first time I was ever in one of these voluntarily

DA:
Will yis all give over I'm trying to get some sleep

CAL:
Goodnight Da.

DA:
Goodnight Cal

MERVYN:
Goodnight Uncle Andy

UNCLE ANDY:
Goodnight Mervyn

CAL:
Goodnight Uncle Andy

UNCLE ANDY:
Goodnight Cal

CAL:
Goodnight Big Mervyn

MERVYN:
Goodnight Cal
(PAUSE)
Goodnight Da.

DA:
Aw for crying out loud. Goodnight Cal,
Goodnight Uncle Andy, Goodnight
Mervyn, Goodnight everybody in bloody
Ballykissangel.

FX WALTONS 3 NOTE "STING"

**WE SEE THE LIGHT OF THE
LANDROVER GO OUT**

**SCENE 38 MORNING NEXT DAY
EXT BALLYKISSANGEL.**

**WE SEE BILLY, MA AND EMER
LOOKING DOWN AT SOMETHING.
I.E. THE CAMERAS POINTING UP AT
THEIR FACES.**

MA:
Would you look at that. Isn't that
lovely?

**SCENE 39 MORNING IMMEDIATELY
LATER INT BACK OF LANDROVER**

**CAL, DA, UNCLE ANDY AND BIG
MERVYN ARE LYING SOUND
ASLEEP. THEY ARE LYING ON
TOP OF EACH OTHER. CAL IS
HOLDING THE SASH TO HIS FACE
LIKE A COMFORT BLANKET.**

BILLY:
(OFF CAMERA)
Should we wake them up?

SCENE 40 MORNING IMMEDIATELY LATER EXT OUTSIDE LANDROVER.

MA PUSHES THE LANDROVER DOOR SHUT.

MA:
No I've a better idea. Let's re-route them.

BILLY, EMER AND MA MAKE FOR THE FRONT OF THE LANDROVER.

SCENE 41 SAME DAY LATER EXT DOCK OR PIER

MA BILLY AND EMER LOOKING OUT TO SEA

EMER:
Aren't you supposed to bring that landrover back?

BILLY:
Nah, I'll tell them I wrote it off – that's what we usually do.

SCENE 42 SAME DAY IMMEDIATELY LATER

EXT SHOT OF FERRY PULLING OUT TO SEA WE HEAR THE VOICES OF DA, BILLY, UNCLE ANDY AND BIG MERVYN.

DA:
Cal wake up! Somebodys put us on a boat

BIG MERVYN:
What are we going to do Uncle Andy?

UNCLE ANDY:
We'll do what loyal Orangemen have always done. March.

CAL:
The concerned passengers of Stena Sealink object to any sectarian march on this.......

FX SOUND FADES DOWN

FX ROLL CREDITS AND TITLE MUSIC.

Cal

Origins

Cal is a child of the Troubles. The only problem is he never grew up. Da, with tears in his eyes, tells the story of how Cal was once selected for a cross-community holiday to Florida but turned it down because he'd miss the internment night riots. Nowadays, Cal is still getting used to the idea that a bus is for getting you from A to B and not for putting across the road and torching it.

With this background you'd be wrong to think of Cal as a juvenile delinquent. From childhood to the present day he does everything his Da tells him to do. Very few fathers today can make that boast.

Politics

Whilst the last thirty years were pretty grim for most people, for Cal they were the 'wonder years'. But recent developments have left Cal feeling confused. In the good ol' days things were simple. Then it was 'Brits out!' now it's 'Brits kind of in but with cross-border bodies and an equality agenda'. Try fitting that slogan onto a placard with poster paints. While Da slavishly accepts 'Gerry's analysis', Cal has the uncomfortable habit of dragging up the past and embarrassing Da with it. For example, 'But Da, didn't you used to say Gerry's friend, that nice Mr Hume, was leader of the Stoop Down Low Party?' or 'Da, what was Gerry getting at when he said "they haven't gone away, you know"?' or 'Da, see the way you're an Assembly man, well whatever happened to "no return to Stormont"?' It is for this reason that Cal hasn't progressed very far in Sinn Féin. He does, however, have one political ambition – to get a green metal ribbon.

Fashion

As a trendy kid on the block, Cal likes to hang out in his cool Hibernia gear – corduroy slacks, tweed sports jacket, waistcoat and Granda shirt set off by his green nylon ribbon. When not dressing to impress he dresses *University Challenge* casual – *The Simpsons*, *South Park* and *Teletubbies* T-shirts.

#

Q What is your favourite book?

A *Da – A Personal History of Ireland in Nine Volumes*, which I've read twenty times and hope to finish some day. I would also like to let publishers know that manuscripts are *still* available.

Q No, Cal, what really is your favourite book?

A *Before the Dawn*, Gerry Adams's autobiography.

Q Stop it, Cal! What's your favourite book?

A All right it's *Winnie the Pooh and the Blustery Day* but I like Ma to read it to me.

Q What is your favourite foreign country?

A Libya, the time me and Da ow!
. . . That hurt, Da!

Q If you could change one thing about yourself what would it be?

A I'd make myself look like Ronan Keating.

Q What is your favourite night-time entertainment?

A Watching my compilation tape of *Gerry Adams Interviews 1970 to Date*.

Q Which living person do you most admire?

A Well, it's a toss up between Cindy Crawford, Pamela Anderson and Alice McGlade who lives in number 47B Divis Tower.

Da:
Cal he said 'admire' not fancy.

Q Cal, what is your definition of the perfect woman?

A One who will go out with me.

dympna

hard about taking up with her sister Emer's husband but after three minutes she decided, 'Sod it, Billy's the man for me.' Dympna says of Billy: 'He's good-looking, he's fun to be with. We share a lot of interests and 'cos he's a cop he's loaded.' The relationship would be just perfect if only Billy was deaf.

Fashion

Keep it short and keep it tight. Dympna wears skirts so short you'd think they were originally made to be bandages. Not that Billy's complaining. The high heels are something else. Without them Dympna would be the same height as Ma. Dympna has adopted the classic style of the wannabe glamour singer. If you wear this gear you are probably fronting a band called Sexpress or Insatiable and you'd most as likely be called Zara or Xena – but certainly not Dympna.

Origins

Dympna may be taken for an air-headed bimbo but in fact she is the smartest member of the family. She left home as soon as possible to seek a future as a singer in London. Da was disgusted that one of his children would go and 'live among the Brits voluntarily'. In fact such was his shame he had to pretend to his Sinn Féin mates that he'd exiled her for informing. Dympna's singing career did not flourish. This was for a lot of reasons – lack of funds, bad breaks, poor management, playing the wrong venues and . . . she couldn't sing. On returning to Belfast, Dympna's career hit a new low when she failed the auditions for *Let Me Entertain You*. Things have turned round since she met Billy. She had to think long and

Q What is your definition of the perfect man?

A Somebody who is sweet and sensitive, caring and deep. Though a platinum card also helps.

Q How do you feel about Emer in all of this?

A Jealous – her boyfriend lives in Spain and he's got a sports car and a swimming pool.

Q What singer do you model yourself on?

A Well, I think I'm a cross between Mariah Carey, Celine Dion . . .

Cal
And a car alarm.

Dympna
Shut up, Cal.

Q If you could change one thing about yourself, what would it be?

Cal
She'd be a natural blonde.

Dympna
I'm warning you, Cal! It would be my family, definitely my family.

Q Which living person do you most admire?

A Aung San Suu Kyi – the woman who won the Nobel Peace Prize for her pro-democracy campaign in Burma. I love the way she does her nails.

Q What is your definition of the perfect day?

A Getting an audition for *Let Me Entertain You.*

the Sectarian Candidate

VÓTÁIL DA

YOUR LOCAL FRIENDLY
SINN FEINER

Transmission date
25 June 1998

give my head peace

Fade in February 1998. We're in the middle of writing our scripts for the second series, which will be broadcast at the end of May. We've got a small problem. The Good Friday Agreement hasn't happened yet but we've got to decide (1) will there be an agreement? (2) will the referendum say Yes to the agreement? (3) should we get our agent to argue for more money for using our psychic powers to predict the future? We just don't know what to do. We're really stuck. And then Ian Paisley announces he won't be attending the negotiations. So great, yes, even Mystic Meg knows there will be an agreement! Let's write the scripts! And hey, if the agreement goes through, there will be an election so that's episode six sorted.

The Sectarian Candidate became our 'election special' broadcast on the evening of the Assembly elections. It is best remembered for its set piece 'Thriller' graveyard sequence which came about like this. We were sitting writing a scene about Da and Cal wandering through a graveyard and taking down the names of the recently deceased to use their votes. Then Michael and I hit on the idea of the corpses coming to life and reclaiming their franchise. They could then transform Da into a zombie à la Michael Jackson and do a 'Thriller' dance! It was, quite frankly, the stupidest idea we'd ever had but we fell about laughing so much that Tim finally had to give in: 'All right, lads, ruin your careers if you want to.' We then took turns trying out the Vincent Price voice and I got the part (I know my horror films).

Fade in April 1998. We're in a graveyard with polystyrene headstones at three o'clock in the morning. Tim as Da is made up as a zombie with zombies dancing round him to the tune of 'Thriller'. Tim's thinking, my career's ruined. Michael and I are on the floor laughing.

damon quinn

SCENE 1. CITY HALL. EXT. (DAY 1). DAY LIGHT.

OPEN ON A TIGHT SHOT OF DA ON MOBILE PHONE

DA:
Hello is that the emergency services?. Yeah fire brigade please. Hello there's two fellas trapped on top of a large public building. Is there any chance you could come and rescue them.

CAMERA PULLS BACK TO REVEAL CAL AND DA ON TOP OF THE CITY HALL.WITH A HUGE BANNER WITH THE WORDS "BRITS OUT - ULSTER SAYS GO".

WILL THE COUNCIL SEE THE FUNNY SIDE? UNLIKELY

DA:
Well they were protesting on top of the city hall as is their right as nationalists. But unfortunately one of the protestors is a dough brain who has padlocked us out and lost the key.

WE SEE CAL'S HURT REACTION

DA:
Yes that was us on the lunch time news.

But the protest is over so quick as you like please we're due at a press conference at Sinn Fein Headquarters. What do you mean six o'clock? It's freezing up here.

CAL:
(SHOUTING THROUGH MEGAPHONE)
Brits out! And has anybody got a ladder?.

SCENE 1A. CITY HALL. EXT. (DAY 1). DAY LIGHT.

WE CUT TO BILLY STANDING BY HIS LANDROVER LOOKING UP AT DA AND CAL SHAKING HIS HEAD

BILLY:
Aw no how am I going to get them down?

UNCLE ANDYS FACE REARS INTO SHOT

UNCLE ANDY:
Simple Billy shoot them down.

BILLY:
What?

UNCLE ANDY:
Snipers over there and there

BILLY:
Catch a...

UNCLE ANDY GRABS BILLY'S RADIO

UNCLE ANDY:
Get me a swat team now.

BILLY:
Give us that. What are you doing here anyway?

THE CAMERA PULLS BACK TO REVEAL UNCLE ANDY IS ACCOMPANIED BY BIG MERVYN

UNCLE ANDY:
I'm handing in my nomination papers for the Assembly election. We Loyalists must save our country from Sinn Fein IRA domination.

BIG MERVYN:
That's right the octopus of republicanism is spreading it's testicles all over Ulster.

BILLY:
Bollocks.

UNCLE ANDY:
It is time for a great leader to arise from our midst, a man of courage, a man of steel, a man of destiny...

BIG MERVYN:
And until he comes along vote Uncle Andy.

BILLY:
You standing for Assembly? I thought you were against the assembly.

UNCLE ANDY:
We have to stand! This deal that Trimble signed is a bionic United Ireland.

BILLY:
(WEARILY)
Embryonic.

UNCLE ANDY:
What?

BILLY:
Like your brain...

THEY WALK OFF TOWARDS THE ENTRANCE UNCLE ANDY TURNS ROUND AND MIMES SHOOTING A RIFLE AT DA AND CAL.

How could you not vote for
such a handsome man?

Da adopts a statesman-like pose

SCENE 1B. EXT. CITY HALL. EXT. (DAY 1). DAY LIGHT.
WE CUT TO DA AT THE FOOT OF A LADDER WITH A PISSED OFF FIRST FIREMAN. CAL IS STILL BEING GIVEN A FIREMANS LIFT DOWN THE LADDER BY A SECOND FIREMAN

DA:
Aw come on now lads don't be like that – Alright Billy – **(HE HOLD OUT HIS ARMS IN A MATTER OF FACT WAY TO BE HANDCUFFED BY BILLY)** It wasn't a complete waste of time look at those cats we rescued.
THE FIRST FIREMAN PRODUCES A COUPLE OF STIFF AS A BOARD DECEASED CATS.

CAL:
(STILL OVER THE SECOND FIREMANS SHOULDER)
Daddy, daddy, you'll never guess. The key **(HE BRANDISHES THE KEY)** it was in my back pocket all the time!

WE CUT TO A TIGHT GROUND SHOT OF DA WITH THE FIREMAN. CAL FALLS INTO SHOT AS IF HE'S BEEN THROWN OFF THE SECOND FIREMANS SHOULDERS. THE SECOND FIREMAN STEPS INTO FRAME FROM DOWN THE LADDER

SECOND FIREMAN:
Oops.

THE FIREMAN STOMPS OFF
DISSOLVE TO NEXT SCENE

SCENE 2. KITCHEN DIVIS TOWER. INT. (DAY 1). LATER.

DA IS ON THE PHONE

DA:
So Gerry did you see us on the news? ...Good wasn't it...I tell you what Gerry see that fire brigade they are unacceptable. That should be a new Sinn Fein policy disband the fire brigade. Who'll put out the fires? Obviously the policy is at an early stage Gerry....sorry my protest was an embarrassment? Well I'm sorry if true republicans embarrass you in front of your new mate Davy Trimble.

SCENE 3. LIVING ROOM DIVIS TOWER. INT. (DAY 1). DAY LIGHT.

CAL AND MA ARE SITTING TALKING

MA:
Scundered I was. I mean ask yourself what did yous achieve?

CAL:
Quite a lot, I got a ride on a fire engine.

MA:
Oh aye well when are yous up in court?

CAL:
Friday. We're going to sneak up onto the roof hoist the tricolour it'll be brilliant.

ENTER DA

DA:
(EXCITED)
Cal, Cal, my day has come Gerry says I can be a Sinn Fein candidate in this assembly election.

CAL:
The assembly? What happened to "No return to Stormont?"

DA:
This isn't a return to Stormont. I've never been there before.

MA:
You've changed your tune. Last night you staggered in drunk shouting "This deal's a betrayal of the Men of 16".

CAL:
"It copperfastens partition" you said.

MA:
And then you phoned Rory O'Brady and joined Republican Sinn Fein.

DA:
Oh no I didn't did I?

MA:
Rory thought he had a true convert, till you tried to order a Chinese off him.

DA:
It's alright Cal, Gerry has explained it to me. This agreement is transitional.

CAL:
So it is a bionic United Ireland.

DA:
Embryonic! It's finally happened Cal after years of self sacrificing struggle Gerry has at last chosen me for high office. I will be at the centre of the real power.

CAL:
Are you getting on to the army council as well?

DA:
No we have now chosen the path of democracy. Democracy from the Greek demos meaning.

CAL:
Kills all known germs.

DA:
That's domestos you tube ye. No from the Greek demos meaning the people and the Greek rocracy meaning something else. It is my civic duty to serve this community and to give something back.

MA:
What about some weapons?

DA:
(IGNORING HER)
I am standing because I believe the time has come for the two communities to work together in a peaceful atmosphere of mutual respect and forge a future together as equals.

CAL:
I thought it was to stop the Orangies getting in.

DA:
Aye that's what I mean. And guess who I'm standing against – Uncle Andy.

CAL:
Yo!

MA:
Well I'm not voting for ye.

CAL:
Want to bet.

SCENE 4. FRONT DOOR UNCLE ANDY'S HOUSE. EXT. (DAY 2). DAY LIGHT.

OUTSIDE THE FRONT DOOR BILLY IS TRYING TO SHOVE THE DOOR AND GET IN THE DOOR WILL NOT MOVE. EMER IS LOOKING ON

BILLY:
(STRAINING)
No I don't know what's wrong with it it's jammed.

EMER:
You'd think you'd be used to breaking down doors.

PUSHES BILLY ASIDE AND WITH SOME EFFORT, BUT NOT TOO MUCH, SHE PUSHES THE DOOR OPEN.
WE CUT TO INSIDE THE FRONT DOOR. WE SEE A HUGE PILE OF ELECTION LEAFLETS AND MANIFESTOS WHICH BILLY AND EMER HAVE TO WADE THROUGH

BILLY:
(TO UNCLE ANDY)
Well thanks for opening the door. Why didn't pick up all this election rubbish.

UNCLE ANDY:
Because somewhere in that pile is a manifesto for Sinn Fein/IRA and I will have no truck with the enemies of Ulster.

BILLY:
You mean you're a lazy scut.
(HE SITS DOWN AND STRETCHES)
Emer get them cleared would ye.

EMER:
(LIFTING A PILE OF LEAFLETS TO DUMP)
I hate elections they're so divisive.

UNCLE ANDY:
No they're not.

EMER:
Yes they are.

UNCLE ANDY:
No they're not... So Billy I trust I can rely on your vote.

BILLY:
Well what's your policies?

UNCLE ANDY:
Loyalist.

BILLY:
and...

UNCLE ANDY:
Is that not enough? That should get me in on the first count.

BILLY:
No I mean have you got a manifesto?

UNCLE ANDY:
Indeed I do. Mervyn and I have worked tirelessly to come up with
a raft of policies with a wide appeal
for my electorate.

UNCLE ANDY PRODUCES HIS "MANIFESTO" IT IS A UNION JACK WITH "VOTE UNCLE ANDY" ON IT.

BILLY:
That's just a Union Jack.

UNCLE ANDY:
The other side.

BILLY FLIPS OVER THE MANIFESTO IT IS THE ULSTER FLAG WITH THE WORD "NO" WRITTEN ON IT.

BILLY:
(READING IT)
No. No to what?

UNCLE ANDY:
No to everything. No to talks with Sinn Fein , no to Dublin, no rerouting....

BILLY:
It's a teensy bit negative.

UNCLE ANDY:
Excuse me my "no" campaign has had a very positive reaction on the doorsteps.

EMER:
Do you not think you should tell the electorate what you're going to say yes to.

UNCLE ANDY:
That's a good idea. Uncle Andy says

yes to no power sharing, yes to no North South bodies.

BILLY:
Well you're not getting my vote.

UNCLE ANDY:
Lundy.

EMER:
Och Uncle Andy seeing as how your family I'll vote for you.

UNCLE ANDY:
You'll do no such thing.

EMER:
What.

UNCLE ANDY:
And don't be going round saying you're voting for me it could ruin my whole campaign. I mean do I look like John Alderdice. No, no, I am in the vanguard of the third force of Ulster resistance.

BILLY:
(TO EMER)
Notice he didn't mention the Ulster Workers Council.

UNCLE ANDY:
Excuse me. When I am elected to theassembly I will work tirelessly... to wreck it

EMER:

So I take it you won't be accepting a members salary then.

UNCLE ANDY:

Listen – if I have to spend my time bringing down a bionic United Ireland, I want paid for it.

BILLY:

Embryonic! It's an embryonic United Ireland!

UNCLE ANDY:

So you admit it then.

BILLY:

Alright you have got my vote.

EMER IS FLICKING THROUGH THE LEAFLETS.

EMER:

By the time you'd read through all these the election would be over.

UNCLE ANDY:

So what's the opposition saying?

EMER:

I can't find the Sinn Fein one.

UNCLE ANDY:

I'm not talking about them I'm talking about my fellow Unionists. My brothers in the loyalist family. What are them bastards saying?

EMER:

We'll here's David Irvine's.

(SHE PRODUCES THE LEAFLET. WE SEE DAVID ERVINE'S HEAD)
You know as a hairdresser I never understood why he doesn't shave off that little tuft of hair at the front of his baldy head. I mean it's two seconds with a razor and it's gone.

UNCLE ANDY:

He can't he needs it. He's the head of a loyalist fringe party.

THIS IS A TERRIBLE JOKE IT'LL GO DOWN A STORM

THEY ALL LAUGH

EMER:

Oh here's the Sinn Fein one...oh my God it's my Da.

WE SEE A SINN FEIN MANIFESTO WITH DA ON IT. THE PHOTO IS OF HIM ON TOP OF THE CITY HALL. THE SLOGAN READS "VOTAIL DA"

BILLY:
(SHAKING HIS HEAD)
Votail Da.

UNCLE ANDY:
He hasn't a chance. Look at that he can't even spell the word vote.

BILLY AND EMER ROLL THEIR EYES.

SCENE 5. DIVIS TOWER. INT. (DAY 2). DAY LIGHT.

CAL AND DA ARE SITTING IN THE ROOM

CAL:
Ma's been stood at the door an hour now.

DA:
It's her own fault I told her if John Hume comes canvassing round here for the SDLP don't open the door to him.

WE CUT TO FRONT DOOR WAY WHERE MA IS BEING REGALED BY JOHN HUME MA IS LOOKING VERY BORED

HUME:
So I'm convinced that a three stranded process is the only way we can resolve these differences between our peoples...

DAMON WILL HAVE TO PLAY HUME. HE'S THE ONLY ONE WITH ENOUGH CHINS

MA:
(TRYING TO SHUT DOOR)
Well thanks very much Mr Hume.

HUME:
No Ma please let me finish cos I'd like to use some of my important catchphrases like dialogue threatens no one. And the other one about how I said it to the Prime Minister and I'll say to you now on this doorstep that's another and then there's my personal favourite, It's not the land that's divided it's the people

MA:
Well I'll really..

HUME:
No you're going to have to do much better than that because when I start I can't stop I've lost complete control of the sound bite. I could go on for hours about the relationships within these islands and between these islands, these islands that we live on that we all have to share...

MA:
Look I...

HUME:
No don't stop me cos I've now gone into complete overdrive with my speech about ending the conflict and taking the gun out of Irish politics forever. As I said to the Prime Minister and I'll say to you now on your doorstep a glass is either half full or half empty depending upon your interpretation and I'm asking Unionists to think about that. Take a break take a kitkat because chocolate threatens no one.

MA:
(SLAMMING DOOR)
Shut up.

HUME:
(NOW WRESTLING WITH THE DOOR)
As I said to the Toiseach I can't – I can't believe it's not butter

WE CUT TO THE LIVING ROOM DA GETS UP AND SHUTS THE LIVING ROOM DOOR LEADING TO THE FRONT HALL.

DA:
He's spent too much time locked up with David Trimble.

CAL:
Aye but should we not be out canvassing as well?

DA:
He can canvass all he wants but he hasn't got what I've got.

CAL:
you haven't?

DA:
I have.
(PRODUCES A HUGE BOX WITH "THE SINN FEIN CANDIDATE KIT" WRITTEN ON IT)
The Sinn Fein Candidate Kit.

THEY OPEN THE BOX

DA:
It's all here. The suit, the black coat with the metal green ribbon

CAL:
(JEALOUS)
Metal ribbon (REGAINING HIS EXCITEMENT) Has it got the linguagerry tapes?

DA:
It has. In 14 days you too can be fluent in Gerry Adams.

CAL:
(READING THE BOOKLET)
Aw Da it covers everything ; how to deal with awkward questions about the provos, there's a whole section on whataboutery

DA HAS ALREADY PUT THE
TAPE ON WE HEAR THE VOICE
OF GERRY ADAMS

ADAMS VOICE OVER:
A chara. Congratulations you are now
the proud owner of the Lingua gerry kit.
Follow this guide and your election is as
inevitable as a United Ireland. Along
with your suit, coat and ribbon you will
find an important looking folder.

DA GETS THER FOLDER
FROM THE BOX

ADAMS VOICE OVER:
This is for carrying your papers the Irish
News, an Phoblact, Radio Times
although a TV Quick is also acceptable.
The Newsletter is of course right out.
Tuck the folder under the right arm and
make sure you have it with you at all
times. This will make you look
businesslike and really dead important.

DURING THE ABOVE SPEECH WE
SEE CAL LOOK AND DISCOVER
EACH OF THE PAPERS EXCEPT
THE RADIO TIMES HE IS RELIEVED
THAT GERRY ACCEPTS T.V QUICK
WHICH HE HAS A COPY OF.
DA POSES AS GERRY SPEAKS

SCENE 5A. DIVIS TOWER. INT. (DAY 2). LATER.

FADE OUT FADE IN DA IS NOW
DRESSED IN ALL THE GEAR FROM
THE KIT BUT STILL LISTENING TO
THE GERRY ADAMS TAPE.

ADAMS VOICE OVER:
..if that happens never worry it's only
UTV. Now lets continue with some more
basic phrases you can use in your
interviews. Repeat after me, Sinn Fein
is not the IRA

FX BEEP

CAL:
What?

DA:
Shut up. ...Sinn Fein is not the IRA

ADAMS VOICE OVER:
I notice you didn't interrupt David
Trimble.

FX BEEP

DA/CAL:
I notice you didn't interrupt David
Trimble.

ADAMS VOICE OVER:
I am absolutely pissed off

FX BEEP

DA/CAL:
I am absolutely pissed off.

ADAMS VOICE OVER:
No the point is the point is..I am trying to answer that question Kirsty however no please let me finish. The point is well let us, let us Kirsty you can shout over me or I can answer the question...now Sinn Fein want to move the peace process forward. Now Kirsty are you going to let me f inish. The point is the point is the point is...

DA AND CAL QUIZZICALLY LOOK AT THE TAPE.

DA:
Is that tape stuck?

MA COMES IN AND SWITCHES OFF THE TAPE

MA:
Jesus I wish they'd bring the media ban back.

CAL:
Do you mind.

MA:
Look at the state of this place. This is a living room not Connolly House. And have you done them dishes?

CAL:
Not yet.

MA:
They haven't gone away you know.

DA:
You stupid woman we haven't got time for dishes we are fighting a crucial election that could determine the political future of this whole island.

CUT HARD TO NEXT SCENE

SCENE 6. DIVIS TOWER. INT. (DAY 2). LATER.

DA AND CAL ARE DOING THE DISHES ONE IS DRYING AND ONE WASHING UP. THEY ARE BOTH WEARING MARIGOLDS. MA IS STANDING OVER THEM. DA IS HOLDING UP A CASSEROLE DISH

DA:
Look Ma – I got rid of those stubborn burnt on stains

MA:
Now yous can go.

DA:
Right Cal time to go out and meet the voters.

SHARP CUT TO NEXT SCENE

SCENE 7. GRAVEYARD. EXT. (DAY 2). DAY LIGHT.

A PRIEST IS READING THE FUNERAL SERMON

PRIEST:
I am the resurrection and the life
He who believeth in me
DA LEANS INTO SHOT

DA:
Excuse me father.

PRIEST:
What?

DA:
What was his name?

THE PRIEST WHISPERS THE NAME INTO DA'S EAR

PRIEST:
He who believeth in me.

DA:
And the address?

WE CUT TO DA AND CAL WALKING ALONG THE GRAVEYARD AWAY FROM THE FUNERAL CAL IS HOLDING THE REGISTER

CAL:
Yup he's on the register.

DA:
Well put him down for us. What about him.

DA POINTS TO THE GRAVE STONE CAL SCURRIES OVER TO THE GRAVESTONE

CAL:
(MUTTERING TO HIMSELF)
In loving memory to... [mumble mumble] ... who departed this life
7 January Nineteen Eighty...

DA:
Oh I know him. He's solid he votes for us all the time.

CAL:
(NOTICING SOMETHING)
Look Da. There's a fresh one over there.

DA AND CAL SCURRY TOWARDS IT AND TAKE NOTES

DA:
That's another one for Sinn Fein

UNCLE ANDY'S VOICE:
Clear off I'm no Sinner.

WE NEED A HEARSE HERE →

DA AND CAL LEAP BACK IN HORROR. UNCLE ANDY AND BIG MERVYN POP UP FROM BEHIND THE GRAVESTONE. BIG MERVYN IS ALSO CARRYING AN ELECTORAL REGISTER

UNCLE ANDY:
How dare you denigrate the democratic process by stealing votes.

BIG MERVYN:
This mans a loyalist and he's voting for us.

DA:
Excuse me what's his address there Cal?

CAL:
He's right on the peace line Number 48.

DA:
(DISAPPOINTED)
Aw no he is one of theirs.

DA AND CAL MAKE TO GO OFF. UNCLE ANDY CALLS AFTER THEM

UNCLE ANDY:
And here you needn't bother mouching around that Jewish plot they're all voting for us.

CAL:
So. We got the Chinese community.

DA:
(POINTING AND SHOUTING EXCITEDLY)
New arrival.

DA AND CAL RUN AFTER IT UNCLE ANDY AND BIG MERVYN FOLLOW AFTER THEM

ALL:
Mine/ we saw it first/ me arse/ etc.

SCENE 8. GRAVEYARD. EXT. (DAY 2). NIGHT.

CAL AND DA ARE STILL GATHERING VOTES. HAS A TORCH AND IS LOOKING AT A GRAVESTONE. IT IS VERY LATE AND CAL IS GETTING A BIT SPOOKED

CAL:
Da could we not go home.

DA:
Just a few more to do Cal.

CAL:
I don't know Da it's getting a bit spooky.

I'M CAN'T DANCE!! WHERE ARE WE GOING TO FIND A bit of a GLIPE? WHO CAN?

SCENE 8A. GRAVEYARD. EXT. (DAY 2). NIGHT.

WE SEE WHERE CAL'S TORCH IS ILLUMINATING THE GRAVEYARD. WE SEE A HAND EMERGE QUICKLY FROM THE GRAVE. IT GRABS CAL'S FOOT. CAL PULLS AWAY, THEN

THE WHOLE ZOMBIE SITS UP. THEN A FEW OTHER ZOMBIES EMERGE FROM BEHIND THE HEADSTONES.

CAL:
(TUGGING DA'S ARM)
Da! Da!

← LETS GET DA'S ARM TO PALL OFF

WE SEE NOW THAT DA HAS BEEN TRANSFORMED INTO A ZOMBIE AND IS STARING WILDLY AT CAL. THE ZOMBIES AND DA START A BRIEF DANCE ROUTINE A LA MICHAEL JACKSON'S THRILLER WITH THRILLER TYPE MUSIC THEY THEN MOVE MENACINGLY TOWARDS CAL

WE CUT TO SHARP TO NEXT SCENE

SCENE 9. CAL'S BEDROOM DIVIS TOWER. INT. (DAY 3). NIGHT.

CAL WAKES UP AND SCREAMS. HE GETS UP AND RUNS OUT OF THE ROOM

Da and Cal meet some 'don't knows' in the graveyard

CUT TO NEXT SCENE

SCENE 10. LIVING ROOM DIVIS TOWER. INT. (DAY 3). NIGHT.

A DISHEVELLED DA AND MA HAVE BEEN WOKEN BY A TERRIFIED CAL

DA:
What's the matter Cal!?

CAL:
It was horrible Da. We were in the graveyard and there was all these zombies coming after me and saying "You took our votes! You took our votes"...and they were all Alliance Party voters! Da we have to put them back.

MA:
That's the fifth time this week he's had that nightmare. Never you take him down that graveyard again.
CUT TO NEXT SCENE

SCENE 11. UNCLE ANDY'S HOUSE. INT. (DAY 3). NIGHT.

UNCLE ANDY ON THE PHONE

UNCLE ANDY:
Mervyn for the last time there's no such thing as zombies, unless you count Seamus Mallon. It's just a nightmare now go back to sleep.

HANGS UP PHONE THINKS PICKS IT UP AGAIN AND DAILS.

UNCLE ANDY:
Hello is that Luigi's pizzas. Still serving? Good I'd like 50 pizzas please; assorted toppings. Yeah it's for the Sinn Fein election head quarters, yeah 47 A Divis Tower. Ask for Da he's the man with the money.

UNCLE ANDY LAUGHS TO HIMSELF AND GOES TO MAKE UP THE STAIRS THE DOOR BELL GOES.

UNCLE ANDY:
Oh it's two o'clock in the morning.
HE OPENS THE DOOR TO REVEAL A CHINESE MAN LOADED DOWN WITH CHINESE CARRY OUTS

CHINESE MAN:
You order the chinese?

UNCLE ANDY:
Wha?

CHINESE MAN:
60 Chinese dinner for Uncle Andy's election campaign.

UNCLE ANDY:
Oh no the dirty

CHINESE MAN:
(SHOUTING DOWN THE STREET)
Miss Golightly, bring in the prawn crackers.

SCENE 12. UNCLE ANDY'S HOUSE. INT. (DAY 4). BREAKFAST TIME. BILLY AND UNCLE ANDY ARE AT THE TABLE

BILLY:
What's for breakfast love?

ENTER EMER WITH TWO MOUNDS OF CHINESE FOOD.

EMER:
King prawn curry with egg fried rice.
(SHE GIVES ONE PLATE TO UNCLE ANDY)

And you're getting the sweet and sour pork. **(HANDS OVER THE PLATE)** Soy sauce anyone?

BILLY IS DISGUSTED BY THE SIGHT

UNCLE ANDY:
This is your Da's fault with his dirty tricks campaign.

EMER:
Yeah well he's been eating pizza for a week. I'll just go and get my Peking duck.

UNCLE ANDY:
(IN A HURRIED WHISPER)
Billy, Billy. Do you know anybody in the drugs squad?

BILLY:
Aye.

UNCLE ANDY:
You couldn't score us some marijuana?

BILLY:
What.

UNCLE ANDY:
It's not for me it's for Da. I'm going to plant it on him .And I thought you lads could stop and search him. He'd be finished.

BILLY:
(OUTRAGED)
Uncle Andy I don't believe I'm hearing this. Do you think the RUC would be involved in framing people?!

UNCLE ANDY GIVES HIM A WRY LOOK

SCENE 13. BELFAST STREET. EXT. (DAY 4). DAY LIGHT.

WE START CLOSE UP ON UNCLE ANDY HE IS IN A VEHICLE SPEAKING INTO A TANNOY BIG MERVYN IS BESIDE HIM DRIVING. A TINNY VERSION OF THE GREEN GRASSY SLOPES IS PLAYING

UNCLE ANDY:
(INTO TANNOY)
Vote Uncle Andy at the assembly election this Thursday.

BIG MERVYN:
Uncle Andy will Billy not mind us borrowing his landrover?
CUT TO EXTERIOR SHOT OF THE LANDROVER FESTOONED WITH UNION JACKS ULSTER FLAGS

WITH A SPEAKER ON TOP. WE RETURN TO THE INTERIOR

UNCLE ANDY:
No, Billy won't mind

BIG MERVYN:
How come?

UNCLE ANDY:
He doesn't know.
(SPEAKING INTO THE MIC AGAIN)
Remember the future's bright the future is Orange with Uncle Andy. Uncle Andy your local no man.

SCENE 13A. STORMONT BUILDINGS. EXT. DAY LIGHT.

CLOSE UP ON DA AND CAL

DA:
What do you think Cal?

CAL:
I don't know – I think it'll look better round the back.

THE CAMERA PULLS BACK TO REVEAL DA AND CAL IN FRONT OF

CARSONS STATUE - STORMONT BUILDINGS IS IN THE BACKGROUND

CAL:
We'll need to put something in its place.

DA:
What about one of Gerry?

DA DOES THE CARSON POSE

DA:
Time to step up the campaign Cal.

DA AND CAL GET INTO A BLACK TAXI

TAXI DRIVER:
This meter's still running mate.

DA:
(TO CAL)
Meter!? I told you to get a Falls Road black taxi!!

SCENE 14. UNCLE ANDY'S HOUSE. INT. (DAY 4). DAY LIGHT.

THE HOUSE IS FESTOONED WITH ELECTION BUNTING AND POSTERS AND DOMINATED BY A HUGE PICTURE OF UNCLE ANDY WITH THE WORD "NO" EMBLAZONED ON IT. BILLY AND EMER ARE WATCHING TELEVISION. BIG MERVYN AND UNCLE ANDY COME IN THE FRONT DOOR. THEY ARE WEARING THEIR ELECTION ROSETTES. BILLY LEAPS UP AND SQUARES UP TO THEM.

BILLY:
Uncle Andy what have I told you before about taking that landrover.

UNCLE ANDY:
There was a time when the RUC would have been only to glad to help their local loyalist candidate.

BILLY:
Aw no you haven't been using it for canvassing. The sergeant's going to go buck mad. You know he's DUP.

BIG MERVYN:
It's alright it's useless anyway. See every time we offered someone a lift to the polling station they screamed and ran away.

EMER:
So are you going to win then?

UNCLE ANDY:
I confidently predict a landslide because I fought this campaign on the issues..

BIG MERVYN:
That's right we kept the personalities out of it.

BILLY:
(DISPARAGINGLY)
Very wise.

BIG MERVYN:
By Thursday it'll be Assemblyman Uncle Andy

UNCLE ANDY:
I've already got my gracious acceptance speech ready Mervyn wait till you hear this. "Madam returning officer, fellow candidates now is not the time for triumphalism. Up yours Da I won. **(HE DOES THE FINGERS)** Then its a quick blast of the sash and a victory cavalcade to the kneebreakers.

BILLY:
Martin Luther King eat your heart out.

EMER:
Uncle Andy you're on the TV.

THEY LOOK AT THE TV AND WE SEE THE TV REPORT. WE SEE A

PICTURE OF UNCLE ANDY WITH THE WORD SLEAZE WRITTEN ACROSS IT.

SCENE 14A. STUDIO B. INT. (DAY 4). LATER.

WILL SHE DO IT FOR NOTHING?

ALISON COMYN:
And we've just heard that one of the candidates in the assembly election, Uncle Andy, is at the centre of sleaze allegations.

LORETTA:
Yes I was sexually harassed by Uncle Andy. He tried to touch me on the **(SHE MOUTHS THE WORD)** His whole campaign is based on no but he would not take no for an answer.

ALISON COMYN:
(GIVES SHUDDER OF DISGUST)
Gives you the creeps doesn't it. Now the weather....

SCENE 14. UNCLE ANDY'S HOUSE CONTD... INT. (DAY 4).

WE CUT BACK TO UNCLE ANDY'S THERE IS A LONG UNCOMFORTABLE PAUSE AS THEY ALL LOOK AT UNCLE ANDY

UNCLE ANDY:
It's all lies it's a conspiracy.

EMER:
Oh aye like a woman would make up allegations like that for no reason.

WE CUT SHARP TO NEXT SCENE

SCENE 15. DIVIS TOWER. INT. (DAY 4). DAY LIGHT.

DA IS PAYING LORETTA MONEY COUNTING THE NOTES INTO HER HAND

DA:
Brilliant performance Loretta now I'll not have to look at his ugly bake across the floor of Stormont. That's half now and the other half as soon as I'm elected.

CUT TO NEXT SCENE

SCENE 16. UNCLE ANDY'S HOUSE. INT. (DAY 4). DAY LIGHT.

UNCLE ANDY:
Aw come on give me the benefit of the doubt. I mean do I look like a sleazy grotty sexual harraser?

HE RECEIVES NO REPLY THEY CONTINUE TO LOOK AT HIM

UNCLE ANDY:
I mean do I look like the type of man to try it on with anything in a skirt? Or the type of man who when he was on a bus would put his hand down on the seat when the woman went to sit beside him and then pretend it was an accident?.. **(NOW FLOUNDERING)** or the kind of man who- who- who would take his dog for a walk down where the nurses flats are so he can look up at the one who changes in the window with no blinds drawn? or ,or, or, the kind of man who would maybe hang around outside Methody about 3.30 when the six form girls get out? Do I look like that kind of man?

THERE IS A SHORT PAUSE

EMER:
Billy I need a bath
(TO UNCLE ANDY) and I'm
locking the door.

BILLY:
Uncle Bill Clinton

UNCLE ANDY:
Mervyn you got to believe me.

BIG MERVYN:
Uncle Andy this is going to bring you
down in the estimation of the punters.

BILLY NODS HIS ASCENT

BIG MERVYN:
You couldn't even pull an oul tugboat
like Loretta.

BILLY LOOKS ASKANCE.

**THE DOOR BELL GOES. UNCLE
ANDY OPENS THE DOOR HE IS
CONFRONTED BY A BATTERY OF
CAMERA'S FLASHING. WE SEE
OUTSIDE UNCLE ANDY'S FRONT
DOOR**

IT'LL SAVE MONEY IF THE GANG PLAY THE REPORTERS

REPORTER:
Uncle Andy what have you got to say
about these sex allegations?

UNCLE ANDY:
They're not true. I never met that
woman before in my life.

REPORTER:
She says you've got a distinguishing
feature.

UNCLE ANDY:
Well I'll prove that's not true.

**UNCLE ANDY GOES TO UNZIP HIS
FLIES. THE CAMERAS FLASH**

REPORTER:
She meant the moustache!

**SCENE 17. HEADLINES SEQUENCE.
INT.**

**WE CUT TO BELFAST TELEGRAPH
HEADLINE WITH A PHOTO OF
UNCLE ANDY IN THE
COMPROMISING POSITION AT THE
FRONT DOOR. HEADLINE READS
"UNCLE ANDY EXPOSED". WE SEE
A NEWS LETTER WITH SIMILAR
PHOTO ONLY WITH A BLACK**

SQUARE AND THE WORD "NO" OVER HIS CROTCH. HEADLINE READS "UNCLE ANDY, NO!"

SCENE 18. BELFAST CITY COUNCIL. INT. (DAY 5). DAY LIGHT.

IT IS ELECTION DAY UNCLE ANDY IS STANDING WITH THE ELECTORAL OFFICER ALONGSIDE BIG MERVYN. EMER AND MA ARE THERE AS WELL

UNCLE ANDY:
I demand a recount.

EMER:
This is the seventy eighth recount Uncle Andy

UNCLE ANDY:
It is my democratic right.

ELECTORAL OFFICER:
Alright, alright I'll count them again. One, two three for Uncle Andy.

THE CAMERA PANS TO THE HUGE PILE FOR DA

ELECTORAL OFFICER:
(VERY PISSED OFF)
Five thousand, six hundred and twenty nine votes to Da. I declare Da the winner.

MA:
Aw God do you have to?

UNCLE ANDY:
I demand a recount.

ELECTORAL OFFICER:
No!

UNCLE ANDY:
It is my democratic right...

EMER:
Uncle Andy you only got three votes and one of them was spoiled.

MA:
The electoral officer only gave it to you because he felt sorry for you.

EMER:
You'd have had four if you'd let me vote for you.

CUT TO NEXT SCENE

SCENE 19. BELFAST CITY COUNCIL. INT. (DAY 5). DAY LIGHT.

ACCEPTANCE SPEECH OF DA AT THE COUNT A BATTERY OF MICS ARE IN FRONT. HE IS ACCOMPANIED BY CAL. THE CAMERAS ARE CLICKING. MA, EMER ,UNCLE ANDY AND MERVYN ARE AT THE BACK OF THE HALL WATCHING

DA:
A chara agus an caed mile failte agus an hig an shig

WE SEE MA AND EMER'S EMBARRASSED REACTION

DA:
agus an Willy wonkas chocolate factory.

CAL:
What?

DA:
(TO CAL)
It's alright it's the Irish bit nobody understands it. (RESUMING SPEECH) I am delighted to be elected to Stormont. Or as we plan to rename it aras an up the provos. But me let me reassure Unionists that all we seek is parity of esteem.Two flags will fly from the Stormont Castle. The tricolour and the, the, the,

CAL:
the starry plough.

DA:
(GIVES CAL A HARD LOOK)
Just a Sinn Fein joke there. It will of course be the tricolour and the Union Jack. This is in fact the tricolour
(DA SHOWS A NORMAL FLAG SIZED TRICOLOUR)

CAL:
And this is the union jack

CAL PRODUCES TINY UNION FLAG

BIG MERVYN:
Right that's it.

MERVYN IS ABOUT TO LUNGE AT THEM BUT UNCLE ANDY RESTRAINS HIM

UNCLE ANDY:
No. No. Do not let yourself be provoked Mervyn. This calls for a dignified response

CUT HARD TO NEXT SCENE

SCENE 20. BELFAST CITY HALL. EXT. (DAY 5). DAY LIGHT.

UNCLE ANDY AND BIG MERVYN ARE ON TOP OF THE CITY HALL THROWING TINS AND MISSILES DOWN. THEY HAVE A BANNER "ANDY SAYS NO". THEY ARE SHOUTING SLOGANS AND ABUSE

SCENE 21. BELFAST CITY COUNCIL. INT. (DAY 5). DAY LIGHT.

THE ELECTORAL OFFICER IS CLEARING UP AFTER THE COUNT. LORETTA COMES IN

LORETTA:
Is Assemblyman Da about?

ELECTORAL OFFICER:
No he's outside dealing with some disturbance.

LORETTA:
Aye well he says for me to call in here today and get my election money.

ELECTORAL OFFICER:
Your...election money?

SCENE 22. BELFAST CITY HALL. EXT. (DAY 5). DAY LIGHT.]

DA AND CAL ARE LOOKING UP AT UNCLE ANDY'S PROTEST. BILLY IS OUTSIDE WITH THE LANDROVER. MA AND EMER ARE ALSO STANDING ABOUT

DA:
Disgraceful.

CAL:
No respect for public property. Will I get the fire brigade then?

DA:
No you're alright Cal.
(TO BILLY) Billy shoot them down.

BILLY:
What?

DA:
It's an abuse of public property.
Contrary to the laws.

BILLY:
What law?

DA:
It'll be passed at the first assembly meeting.

THE ELECTORAL OFFICER ARRIVES WITH LORETTA IN TOW

ELECTORAL OFFICER:
Assemblyman Da. I formally declare your election null and void.

DA:
What for?

ELECTORAL OFFICER:
Oh for a start bibery, corruption, misuse of electoral funds to conduct a smear campaign, fraud...

CAL:
Not for stealing the votes of the dead?

ELECTORAL OFFICER:
No you all do that. Constable arrest this man.

BILLY DOES SO WITH THE HANDCUFFS

BILLY:
Come on Da You know the routine.

DA:
I have the right to remain silent if however...

BILLY LEADS DA TO THE BACK OF THE LANDROVER

MA:
Thank god that's another election over. That was the worst yet.

ELECTORAL OFFICER:
Afraid not madam. This means there'll have to be an election.

CAL:
I'm standing!.
Vote me in to get him out!.

WE SEE MA, EMER ET AL'S REACTION

WHY NOT CUT SCENES 21 & 22 AND LET DA WIN? WE COULD GET SOME ASSEMBLY PLOTS FOR SERIES 3!!

SCENE 23. TOP OF CITY HALL. EXT. (DAY 5). DAY LIGHT.

WE SEE UNCLE ANDY AND BIG MERVYN. BIG MERVYN IS LOOKING SHEEPISH. UNCLE ANDY ON A MOBILE PHONE.

UNCLE ANDY:
....Yeah. Fire Brigade, please. Hello there's two fellas trapped on top of a large public building. Is there any chance you could come and rescue them?

emer

THE INTERVIEW

said "cow",' says Billy. When Emer left, Billy swore he'd never look at another woman. Fifteen minutes later he was snogging the face off Dympna on Ma's couch in Divis Tower. But up until now we've never heard Emer's side of the story. Well here it is, but as Billy says, 'If you believe this you're a bigger sap than I was.'

As everyone knows, Emer and Billy's marriage was 'a beacon of hope for our two divided communities'. The fact that the marriage broke up in acrimony when Emer ran off with Spanish Lothario, Ronaldo, doesn't augur well for future cross-community relations. However broken-hearted, Billy wasn't bitter. As he said, 'Ours was a unique special love but at the end of the day I couldn't hold on to her 'cos she was a lying, cheating, conniving, back-stabbing cow!' With the passing of time he has mellowed. 'Maybe I shouldn't have

emer

Emer, why did the marriage break up?

There's all sorts of reasons why people grow apart. It can happen almost imperceptibly at first. Little things that over time become a huge chasm between two people. The fact that Ronaldo was a rich, gorgeous, exotic Spanish hunk who gave me the best sex I'd ever had in my life was nothing to do with it.

But instead of running off to Spain shouldn't you have stayed in Belfast and tried to work it out?

Get real.

Where does that leave your passionate commitment to peace and reconciliation in Northern Ireland?

I feel I can achieve more for the cause of peace in Northern Ireland here in Spain. Besides, if I'd had to stay and look at Uncle Andy's horrible sectarian Proddy Orange bake for another day I'd have decked him.

So what do you do in Spain?

Well, I had a hairdressing salon in Fuengirola but it got closed down after an incident involving Julio Iglesias. Julio, if you're reading this, I honestly don't know how that Immac got into the shampoo but they do some great wigs these days.

What do you miss most about home?

Em . . . can I get back to you on that one?

How did you feel about Billy taking up with Dympna?

Well, as the younger sister Dympna used to get all my hand-me-downs, it didn't surprise me when I heard. Got to go now – I've just seen Julio Iglesias!

Saving
ryan's daughter

Transmission date
28 May 1999

give my head peace

The one where twenty-three identical Ryan brothers intimidate Cal into marrying their sister and Uncle Andy learns to walk like a Catholic.

Saving Ryan's Daughter was written in two and a half days in a secluded cottage outside Bryansford, County Down. It would have been written in two days except we got very drunk in Jim Lewsley's bar in Newcastle and spent most of the next morning downing Alka Seltzers and wishing Jim Lewsley hadn't hired a karaoke machine. Once we sobered up we realised we had a good plot outline.

We had been toying with the idea of a shotgun wedding for Cal. He seemed the obvious candidate, never having had a girl before. We liked the idea of mad Seamus Ryan from south Armagh and his huge family of lookalike sons intimidating Cal into marrying his pregnant daughter. The trouble was, how to save Cal from getting hitched at the altar. We thought of making Uncle Andy the father, but this created its own problems until Michael had the bright idea of a double for Uncle Andy. All we had to do was to lay the seeds of a doppelgänger early in the episode and reveal all at the end.

In all we ended up with twenty-three Ryan brothers – twelve appearing in Divis Tower to welcome Cal into the family, another seven or eight to ring Cal on his stag night (most of this scene was cut for reasons of time) and at the actual wedding we had a couple more just for good luck.

As usual the Hole in the Wall Gang likes to court controversy. The interior wedding scenes were shot in Bishop Pat Buckley's church in Omeath, County Louth. For some reason every church in Northern Ireland seemed reluctant to allow us to use their facilities to film a shotgun wedding featuring a pregnant bride, twenty-three brothers and the singing of 'The Men Behind the Wire'. Bishop Buckley very kindly let us use his church but unfortunately a female priest, ordained by Bishop Buckley, Mother Frances Meigh, turned up during filming and was apparently less than impressed. It's probably just as well we didn't film it in the Vatican.

tim mcgarry

SCENE EP 3/1. DIVIS TOWER. INT. STUDIO. (DAY 1). DAY LIGHT. AFTERNOON.

CAL, DRESSED IN A DRESSING GOWN, IS STARING BLANKLY AT THE TV. MA AND DYMPNA ARE LOOKING ON CONCERNED

DYMPNA:
Ma I'm getting worried about him. He doesn't get out of bed till lunchtime, he never washes and he won't eat anything except Coco Pops

MA:
So what's new.

DYMPNA:
Just sitting there watching countdown

MA:
LOOKING AT THE TV SEXILY MUSING
Wish your Da was like Richard Whitely

DYMPNA:
You wish he dyed his hair?

MA:
No I wish he lived in England.

WE HEAR THE TUNE THAT IS PLAYED ON COUNTDOWN FOR THE 30 SECOND CONUNDRUM THE MUSIC ENDS

CAL:
BORED
Armalite.

DYMPNA:
For Gods sake he looks like death warmed up. It's worse than having Seamus Mallon round for tea.

DA ARRIVES IN

DA:
Come on Cal come on we're late for the rally.

MA:
Thank god he's going out. What is it today?

DA:
Disband the RUC.

DYMPNA:
Oh aye Billy's going to that.

DA:
Great he can give us a lift then

DYMPNA:
No he can not.

DA:
It's on his way.

DYMPNA:
No he's to drop me off at Summertan.

DA:
Typical RUC 93 % Protestant 100% disobliging.
TO CAL
Come on you...what are you doing sitting in your cacks?... The blanket men commemoration march isn't till next Thursday.

MA:
Have you not noticed he's been like that for days.

DA:
LOOKING AT CAL
Alright who told him Linda Bryans is married to Mike Nesbitt.

THERE IS A PAUSE

DYMPNA:
I thought everybody knew that.

DA:
Cal I'm sorry to have to tell you this but even if she wasn't married Linda would be out of your league. Get real son you want to lower your sights.

DYMPNA:
Pamela Ballentine?

DA:
No! Look come on Cal snap out of it we've a rally to go to.

CAL:
I'm not going.

DYMPNA/ DA/ MA:
GASPING

What!

CAL:
Not going.

DA:
Not going you have to go. It's a "Scrap the R.U.C." rally. We're all marching down the road holding letters. You've been picked to carry the U of RUC

HE PRODUCES THE CARD WITH THE LETTER U WRITTEN ON IT

CAL:
You do it.

DA:
I can't I'm holding the S of "scrap"

HE PRODUCES THE CARD WITH THE LETTER S ON IT

CAL:
Well you hold the S and the U then.

DA:
They're on the opposite ends of the street, we're marching eleven abreast I can't be on two footpaths at once. What is it son? What's wrong with ye?

CAL:
24 years...waiting for a chance. To tell her how I feel...maybe get a second glance. Now I've got to get used to not living next door to Alice.

DA:
Alice?

MA/ DYMPNA:
Alice!

DA:
Who the feck is Alice?

Watch the pronounciation!

MA:
The girl lives next door with the terrible teeth.

DYMPNA:
The one who's marrying the dentist.

DA:
Her. Sure you never spoke to the girl.

CAL:
I was waiting for her to make the first move.

DA:
24 years you had to ask that girl out. And you never even spoke to her.

CAL:
I was playing hard to get.

DA:
No, no it doesn't work that way. If you want to get a woman you've got to put yourself out, be witty, charming, flirty and if you think your lucks in maybe get a bit touchy feely.

CAL:
Oh aye you mean the way you are with Barbara De Brun?

DA:
Yes – no.

MA:
What!!!???

SCENE EP 3/2. UNCLE ANDY'S. INT. STUDIO. (DAY 1). DAY LIGHT. AFTERNOON.

THE LIVING ROOM IS A MESS. UNCLE ANDY IS SPRAWLED ON THE TV WATCHING SOME CHILDREN'S CARTOONS. THE LIGHTS ARE DIMMED. BILLY COMES DOWN THE STAIRS GETTING READY TO GO OUT, AND CLOCKS THE MESS

BILLY:
Och look at the state of this place. You said you'd tidy up.

UNCLE ANDY:
I have tidied up.

BILLY:
Uncle Andy.

UNCLE ANDY:
Alright I'll do some dusting when you go off to work.

BILLY:
You won't as soon as I go out that door you'll slob about all day watching TV

UNCLE ANDY:
Aye maybe I should join the RUC and get paid for it.

BILLY:
What did you say?!

UNCLE ANDY:
Nothin

BILLY:
You and me is having a talk when I get home.

UNCLE ANDY:
About what.

BILLY:
About your attitude.

UNCLE ANDY:
There's no point I won't get a word in.

BILLY:
Why?

UNCLE ANDY:
Cos I won't be here.

BILLY:
Why where are you going?

UNCLE ANDY:
Out.

BILLY:
Who with?

UNCLE ANDY:
Friends.

BILLY:
What friends?

UNCLE ANDY:
You wouldn't know them.

BILLY:
Big Mervyn.

UNCLE ANDY:
You checking up on me.

BILLY:
I don't need to I hear enough about ye.

UNCLE ANDY:
Like what?

BILLY:
Well I had your New Dole Officer, Mrs Johnson, ringing me to work and she says you and Big Mervyn have been bunking off your job skills classes.

UNCLE ANDY:
She's a liar.

BILLY:
Aye that's what she does. Executive Officer in the Civil Service spends her day ringing up people and telling lies about their relatives. And you got money off me for bus fares and lunches. No doubt the two of yous are straight down the Kneebreakers with it. Or off embarrassing yourselves down the under 25s disco.

UNCLE ANDY:
You're just jealous.

BILLY:
I would be if you pulled any of them.

UNCLE ANDY:
What do you know. After a woman's been with me she's ruined for any other man.

BILLY:
Too right she's ruined after you, she sees any other man, she runs a mile.

SCENE EP 3/3. DIVIS TOWER; KITCHEN + LIVING ROOM. INT. STUDIO. (DAY 1). DAY LIGHT. EVENING.

DA IS ON THE PHONE TO GERRY IN THE KITCHEN GETTING AN EAR BASHING

DA:
Gerry ...eh sorry for not turning up at the rally bit of a domestic you know. Yes I did see the Telegraph.

WE SEE THE HEADLINE "SINN FEIN SLAMS CATHOLIC CHURCH SHOCKER" UNDERNEATH THERE IS A PHOTO WITH THE MARCHERS CARRYING THEIR LETTERS IT READS "CRAP THE R.C."

DA:
The archbishops been on? Well look on the bright side at least they can't accuse us of being anti Protestant. Don't worry Gerry I'll be at the "no to decommissioning rally" tomorrow. Don't you worry I'll bring the S....There's two S's ? Yes Gerry no problem.
HE HANGS UP
Cal we need another S.

DYMPNA IS COAXING CAL THROUGH THE FRONT LIVING ROOM DOOR WHICH SHE IS HOLDING SLIGHTLY AJAR

DYMPNA:
Trust me Cal you look great.

CAL:
I'm not sure about this

DYMPNA:
It's trendy, the girls will love it.

CAL:
AS HE ENTERS DRESSED AND MADE UP LIKE SHANE OUT OF BOYZONE – WITH LOTS OF FACE AND EAR PIERCING.
Are you sure I look like Shane out of Boyzone?

ENTER

DA:
Alright son. Dympna if you see Cal will you tell him we need another S. Ahhhhhhhh!!!!! What have you done to him?

DYMPNA:
I've given him a complete makeover.

DA:
You did this to him? What's that on his face.

DYMPNA:
Body piercing. Makes him more attractive to women.

DA:
It makes him more attractive to magnets.

DYMPNA:
Just ignore him Cal.

DA:
I tell you if the Provos did that to somebody they'd say it was a breach of the Ceasefire.

DYMPNA:
Don't you listen to him Cal if you take my advice you'll get straight down that disco and wow the women.

CAL:
Wow them?

DYMPNA:
Wow them.

CUT HARD TO NEXT SCENE

SCENE EP 3/4. DISCO. INT. (DAY 1). EVENING.

CAL IS FINISHING HIS PINT AT THE BAR.

CAL:
Wow the women.

CAL COOLY SAUNTERS UP TO A GROUP OF GIRLS. THEY LOOK AT HIM HE LOOKS AT THEM

CAL:
Wow!

THE GIRLS ARE STARTLED A COUPLE OF GIRLS SCREAM ONE DROPS A GLASS. CAL IS UNSUCCESSFUL . HE THEN DANCES UP TO ANOTHER WHO IS ON HER OWN I.E. BERNADETTE

CAL:
Wow!

SHE GIVES HIM A LOOK OF INCOMPREHENSION. CAL TURNS AWAY AND THINKS

CAL:
No doesn't work.

HE SHRUGS AND WALKS TO
THE DISCO EXIT.

CUT TO A SMOOTHLY
DRESSED UNCLE ANDY
SIDLING UP TO THE WOMAN
WHO IS ON HER OWN

UNCLE ANDY:
EXTREMELY SEXILY
Wow.

THE CAMERA PULLS BACK AS
UNCLE ANDY AND THE WOMAN
ON HER OWN START TO
CHAT.

**SCENE EP 3/5. DIVIS TOWER. INT.
STUDIO. (DAY 2). DAY LIGHT.
MORNING.**

CAPTION "2 MONTHS LATER"

CAL, MA AND DYMPNA ARE
WATCHING TV. DA COMES IN
WITH A HUGE PILE OF
LETTERS IN HIS HAND HE
CHUCKS THEM ON THE
FLOOR

DA:
More bloody junk mail. Rubbish
the lot of it. Why do they keep sending
me this crap?

MA:
They're your constituents. You're an
Assembly man.

DA:
Exactly I'm a Assembly man not bloody
Jim'll fix it? I don't know why they call it
an Assembly seat I haven't sat down
since I got elected. Cal file that for me
would ye.

CAL:
No problem Da.

HE PICKS UP A BUNDLE OF
MAIL AND THROWS IT OUT THE
WINDOW

CAL:
Ah this takes me back to my
temporary postman days.

DA:
**PICKING UP THE REMAINDER OF
HIS MAIL AND GOING THROUGH IT**
Oh look I've been specially selected I'm
going to win a quarter of a million
pounds. Must reply to that....
**DISCOVERING SOMETHING ELSE IN
THE MAIL**
A car key, magic.

MA:
Oh look we've been invited to a wedding. Mr and Mrs Seamus Ryan

DA:
Mad Seamus Ryan from Crossmaglen?

MA:
Aye that's where it is. Who is he?

CAL:
Officially he's a valued member of the republican movement unofficially he's a lunatic.

DA:
Let's just say it's thanks to Seamy Ryan South Armagh is the international tourist attraction it is today.

MA:
Well his daughter Bernadette is getting married.

DA:
LAUGHING
I know I heard all about it down the armalite and ballot box. Seemingly the daughter came up to Belfast had a one night stand and got pregnant to some fella. Seamy tried looking for a star in the East, but no luck. So they went looking for a mug in Belfast. And it looks like they've found him.

MA:
So it's like a shotgun wedding.

CAL:
Knowing Seammy Ma it's more of a rocket propelled grenade wedding.

DYMPNA:
That's terrible this is the 90's does the fella have no choice?

DA:
Oh he does and he's wisely chosen to live. Wait till I tell the lads I'm going to that wedding who is the poor sap anyway?

MA:
READING
Cal.

DA:
LAUGHING
God love him...what!
TURNING ON CAL
What in the name of God have you done?

CAL:
I don't know no Bernadette, I didn't do nothing, it wasn't me.

DA:
You're not in Castlereagh now, tell the truth.

CAL:
Alright that night I went out and I did like Dympna told me.

DA:
What was that?

CAL:
I wowed some girls.

DA:
What about Bernadette did you wow her?

CAL:
She might have been called Bernadette I don't know.

DA:
Oh great one night in twenty years I let him go out on his own and who does he tackle, mad Seamy Ryan's daughter.
TURNING ON DYMPNA
This is all your fault.

DYMPNA:
What did I do. All I did was get some nice clothes and a bit of body piercing.

DA:
And this is the result of his body piercing.

[CUT TO NEXT SCENE]

SCENE EP 3/6. DIVIS TOWER KITCHEN, THEN LIVING ROOM. INT. STUDIO. (DAY 2). DAY LIGHT. AFTERNOON.

KITCHEN

DA IS ON THE PHONE

DA:
Gerry.... You're looking forward to the wedding... just on that I've had a chat with Cal and I'm pretty certain, in fact I'm a hundred percent certain that he couldn't possibly be the dad....Oh you know that. Well with the greatest respect Gerry em why does my son have to... Seamy Ryan says somebody has to pay for it. Right I understand difficult stage in the peace process...important to keep South Armagh on board... lunatic... yes. But have you no influence over him?...I see....no, no I don't think anybody's bought them a Cappuccino maker he'd love that.

CUT TO LIVING ROOM, DAY

DA COMES THROUGH THE KITCHEN DOOR

CAL:
Well?

DA:
I've got good news and bad news.

CAL:
What's the bad news.

DA:
You're going to have to marry Ryan's daughter. A woman you neither know nor love. And you'll probably be miserable for the rest of your life.

CAL:
And what's the good news?

DA:
Gerry's getting you a cappuccino maker. Knowing Gerry it'll be top the range it'll do expresso and latte.

CAL:
I don't want to get married Da.

DA:
Son nobody in their right mind wants to get married.

CAL:
Why me? Why me? Why do I have to do it.

DA:
To get us a united Ireland son.

CAL:
What?

DA:
You accept Gerry's analysis that the Peace Process is a vehicle that will lead us inevitably to a United Ireland.

CAL:
Yes

DA:
Well Seamus Ryan says that if his daughter is not married and made respectable. Then he's going to hijack that vehicle, put it across the road and set it on fire. So me and Gerry's asking you do this thing for Ireland.

CAL:
Why me?

DA:
Did Patrick Pearse say "why me?" Did James Connolly say "why me?" as he was tied to a chair and brutally done to death by the British

CAL:
Well they did seize the GPO and start an armed insurrection against the forces of the crown I never even touched the girl so I'm not marrying her.

DA:
Son if you do this you'll take your place among the great Republican Martyrs

CAL:
Don't care.

DA:
If you don't do this the peace process will collapse into chaos and anarchy.

CAL:
So.

DA:
I'll buy you a Sony playstation.

CAL:
Will you get me a copy of Tomb Raider 3.

CUT TO NEXT SCENE

SCENE EP 3/7. UNCLE ANDY'S. INT. STUDIO. (DAY 3). DAY LIGHT. EVENING.

BILLY AND UNCLE ANDY ARE IN THE ROOM

BILLY:
I've a bone to pick with you . I know you may not approve of me and Dympna but that's no excuse for being rude to her.

UNCLE ANDY:
What are you talking about

DYMPNA:
She said hello to you today and you just walked straight past her.

UNCLE ANDY:
Where was this?

DYMPNA:
Marks and Spencers the lingerie section.

UNCLE ANDY:
That wasn't me I've been here all day.

BILLY:
Oh aye like there's two identical greasy haired badly dressed Orange Elvis fanatics wandering round Belfast.

UNCLE ANDY:
It wasn't me alright.

BILLY:
And I suppose it wasn't you that Mrs Johnston saw yesterday pressed up against the window of Anne Summers?

UNCLE ANDY:
It wasn't me.

BILLY:
It was that double of yours again was it.

UNCLE ANDY:
Aye it was.

BILLY:
Yeah I suppose it was him drank all my beer out of the fridge,

UNCLE ANDY:
That might have been me.

DYMPNA COMES IN THE FRONT DOOR

BILLY:
How's Cal bearing up?

DYMPNA:
Didn't get a word out of him

BILLY:
That bad?

DYMPNA:
No he was too wrapped up in his Sony Playstation.

UNCLE ANDY:
[ENJOYING HIMSELF]
Cal's getting married and his girls up the duff. I didn't think he had it in him.

BILLY:
He didn't he's not the father.

UNCLE ANDY:
Ha! I suppose the poor girl can comfort herself with that thought. Oh I can't wait.

DYMPNA:
I didn't think you'd want to go.

UNCLE ANDY:
And miss seeing my fenian one time in laws writhing in misery? It'll be one of the happiest days of my life.

DYMPNA:
PRODUCING THE WEDDING INVITATION FROM HER BAG
You can't go have you not seen the invite

READING

"No Brits, No Peelers, No Agents of the British Crown, No loyalists, No Orangemen, No Unionists, No Protestants, No Castle Catholics, No West Brits, No Free State Irish Traitors, No SDLP, No Conor Cruise O'Brien.

→ no writing it down

BILLY: on the Card make her learn it!

You hear that twelve "no's" in one sentence. These are your kind of people.

UNCLE ANDY:

Well how's he getting to go?

DYMPNA:

He's parking the landrover three streets away and calling himself Liam for the day.

UNCLE ANDY:

Well then I'll just call myself Rory O'Bogtrotter. Shouldn't be too hard to pass myself off as one of them. Just not wash for a week, gurn all day, and act like a big ignorant lazy gobshite who's never worked a day in his life.

DYMPNA:

What do you mean "act".

SCENE EP 3/8. DIVIS TOWER. INT. STUDIO. (DAY 4). DAY LIGHT. EVENING.

CAL IS PLAYING HIS SONY. DA IS REMONSTRATING WITH MA

DA:

Look the two families have to meet before the wedding it's normal

MA:

Aye it's also normal for the groom to meet the bride before he marries her.

DA:

Ryan's says she's not getting out not after what happened the last time.

FX BING BONG

DA:

Now try and be polite and nobody mention the ceasefire.

HE EXITS THROUGH THE HALL DOOR CLOSING IT BEHIND HIM

MA:

Son are you sure you're ready to get married?

CAL:
TOTALLY DISTRACTED BY THE PLAYSTATION
Wha?

MA:
Are you sure you're ready to get married?

CAL:
Oh aye married no problem.

MA:
No I mean are you ready for the commitment, the responsibility the changes it's going make to your life.

CAL:
Changes oh aye...can we have waffles for dinner.

DA COMES BACK THROUGH THE HALL DOOR IN A STATE OF SHOCK

MA:
What?

DA IS FOLLOWED BY SEAMUS RYAN WHO IS DRESSED TOUGH – IN LEATHER JACKET AND ACTS LIKE THE CLASSIC THUG IRA MAN WE HAVE SEEN IN ALL THOSE FILMS. HE IS FOLLOWED IN QUICK SUCCESSION BY A NUMBER (12) OF BURLY YOUNG MEN ALL DRESSED SIMILARLY.

SEAMUS:
Well Da I hope you don't mind I've brought a few of the boys to see you.

DA:
The boys?

SEAMUS:
My sons.

DA:
Oh.

SEAMUS:
This is Paddy Joe, Johnny Joe, Willie Joe, Mickey Joe, Jimmy Joe, Tommy Joe, Timmy Joe, Gerry Joe, Bertie Joe, Mo Joe, Joe Joe and Simon. Where are the twins?

VOICE FROM HALL:
We're out in the hall Da.

MA:
UNCOMFORTABLY
Eh, do yous want a cup of tea?

SEAMUS:
If it's no trouble.

MA EXITS TO KITCHEN TO MAKE TEA

SEAMUS:
Now where is the lucky man?

DA SHEEPISHLY POINTS HIM OUT

SEAMUS:
CLICKING FINGERS
Simon.

SIMON CROSSES TO WHERE CAL IS SWITCHES OFF THE TV . HE PULLS A CHAIR UP AND PUTS HIS FACE UNCOMFORTABLY CLOSE TO CAL'S. CAL IS SURROUNDED BY ALL THE BROTHERS

CAL:
Hello

SIMON:
I've got one thing to say to you. Our only sister Bernadette is very dear to us and we love her and if you do anything to annoy, hurt or upset her we will make you very, very, sorry.

VOICE FROM HALL:
And so will we.

SIMON:
And so will the other brothers who aren't here. That said welcome to the family.

CAL:
SQUEAKING
Thanks.

SIMON GETS UP

SEAMUS:
Well I'm glad we broke the ice. See you at the wedding Da.

HE CLICKS HIS FINGERS, HE AND THE SONS ALL EXIT

DA:
Safe home.

ENTER MA WITH A TEA TROLLEY

MA:
Right who takes sugar? Did they have to rush off?

CAL:
Da will you take the playstation back I don't want it anymore.

DA:
Pre wedding nerves son. Don't worry you'll be fine.

MA:
Well they seemed like a nice family.

DA:
Nice?!

MA:
Pity I didn't get to meet Mrs Ryan where was she?

DA:
Lying exhausted somewhere.

CAL:
Da, Da you've got to get me out of this.

DA:
Sure no problem I'll put an ad in An Phoblacht "Who got Mad Seamus Ryan's daughter up the duff? Would you step forward and let my son Cal off the hook."
SIGHS IN A WORLD WEARY WAY
God but this family gets into all the shit. I'm sick of it. Just sick of it.

HE EXITS PAST THE CAMERA IN THE DIRECTION OF THE AUDIENCE

MA:
Where's does he think he's going?

DA:
SPRINGING BACK IN
Right I'm back there's only one thing to do ...get blind drunk. It's your last night of freedom, son, we're going to get plewtered, strip you naked, chain you to a lamp post and cover you with paint.

CAL:
Is that instead of getting married or as well?

DA:
You're going to have the stag night to end all stag nights.

*Script's too long
Have to lose this
scene*

CUT TO NEXT SCENE
SCENE EP 3/9. DIVIS TOWER. INT. STUDIO. (DAY 5). DAY LIGHT. EVENING.

DA, CAL, UNCLE ANDY AND BILLY ARE SITTING AROUND A SOFA BORED RIGID IN PARTY HATS. THERE IS AN IRONING BOARD AND A PILE OF WASHING IN A WASH BASKET . EVERYBODY IS YAWNING.

MA COMES IN WITH A BOWL OF CRISPS TO BE HANDED ROUND AND GOES BACK TO HER IRONING

It's All GoT To Go UNFORTUNATELY!

MA:
Just you pretend I'm not here.

UNCLE ANDY:
Well if you ask me son marriage is a mugs game. You've got to get the right attitude to woman. You see, for me, a woman is like a fine wine.

CAL:
What do you mean?

HATE LOSING THIS!

UNCLE ANDY:
You gotta get both of them drunk as quick as possible. Don't get involved just love em and leave them.

CAL:
I wouldn't mind but I didn't even get to love em.
CAL GIVES OUT A LONG DEPRESSED SIGH

WE HEAR THE CLOCK, SOMEBODY YAWNS. DA LOOKS AT HIS WATCH

BILLY:
[CRACKING UP]
Aw for God's sake this is the worst stag night I've ever been to. I thought we'd be out on the town raising hell.

CAL:
And miss the Kelly show I think not.

BILLY:
Aw we're not going to watch the Kelly show, it goes on for hours.

DA:
Not it doesn't it, just seems like that.

UNCLE ANDY:
Aye well wake me up when it's over will yous.

BILLY:
Anything else fantastic you'd like to do on your stag night Cal? We could paint the walls and sit and watch it dry.

DA:
It's Cal's night he can do what he wants. That's why I've cancelled the strippagram and we're playing Connect Four later on.

BILLY:
Aw for crying out loud

CAL:
Why what did you do on your stag night?

BILLY:
Stag week. At one point all 35 of us were blind drunk in the middle of the afternoon and ran round the City Hall buck naked in broad daylight..

CAL:
Did the cops not stop ye?

BILLY:
We were the cops. Most of us were on duty.

OUT

DA:
And you wonder why your marriage didn't work out.

CAL:
We know why it didn't work out cos me and you and Uncle Andy...

DA STOPS CAL'S MOUTH

N.B. Look on the bright side. We've now got 2 minutes of the next episode written!

DA:
STANDING UP
Anyway Cal, before Kelly starts I'd just like to make a short speech...

BILLY:
I think I'd rather have Kelly.

DA: *START SCENE HERE*
A short speech about my son Cal here. My daughters lets me down. One after

the other they betrayed me, broke my heart, stabbed me in the back, turned away from their faith, their traditions, their culture, their people, their very souls. Anything that gave them any worth to go out with a peeler.

BILLY:
Could you just get on to the Cal bit please.

DA:
Whereas Cal was a rock. A stalwart. Always there for me except that time when he didn't turn up to carry the U of "Scrap the RUC". But, nobody's perfect – well apart from Gerry Adams – and now like a true Republican he's going to sacrifice himself, marry a woman he doesn't know who has a family that makes the Krays look like the Waltons. I'd just like to say Cal I'm going miss you when you move out of this house.

DA SITS DOWN WITH TEARS IN HIS EYES

CAL:
Thanks Da.....
SUDDENLY PERTURBED
What do you mean move out of the house?

DA:

You're getting married you've to live with your wife.

CAL:

Oh that is brilliant that is just brilliant. I've to move out of the house now that's the next thing.

DA:

Course you do you've to live in South Armagh.

CAL:

Ah no that's it. I'm not doing it. Weddings off.

THE PHONE RINGS DA GETS IT.

DA:

It's for you.

CAL TAKES IT

CUT TO

SCENE EP 3/9A. PHONE BOX IN COUNTRY. INT. (DAY 5). DAY LIGHT. EVENING.

WE SEE ONE BURLY GUY ON THE PHONE. AS HE TALKS THE CAMERA PULLS BACK TO REVEAL A GROUP OF MEN ROUND THE PHONE. THEY ARE ALL DRESSED IN THE LEATHER JACKETS ETC

BURLY GUY:

Hello Cal. I'm Charlie Joe, and I'm speaking on behalf of Vinty Joe, Sorley Joe, Barry Joe, Harry Joe, Sammy Joe and Rupert. We're the other brothers you didn't meet and I just want you to know that what was said goes for us as well.

CUT BACK TO DIVIS TOWER

SCENE EP 3/9B. DIVIS TOWER. INT. STUDIO. EVENING.

CAL:

See you tomorrow .... brother.

SCENE EP 3/10. UNCLE ANDY'S. INT. STUDIO. (DAY 6). DAY LIGHT. MORNING.

BILLY AND DYMPNA ARE GETTING READY FOR THE WEDDING

BILLY IS WEARING A BUTTONHOLE AND DYMPNA IS WEARING A HAT

DYMPNA:
Where's Uncle Andy?

BILLY:
Upstairs making himself into a Catholic.

DYMPNA:
Come on Uncle Andy we're going now.

UNCLE ANDY COMES DOWN THE STAIRS WEARING A GHASTLY VIVID GREEN SUIT HE CARRIES A SHILLELAGH AND HAS A BILLY COCK HAT ON HIS HEAD.

UNCLE ANDY:
SINGING
How are things in glockamara?
AFFECTING SOUTHERN IRISH ACCENT
Top o the morning to you.

BILLY:
What are you doing?

UNCLE ANDY:
I'm blending in. Can we stop off at a farm on the way I won't feel properly dressed until I have a pig under me arm?

BILLY:
KNOCKING HIS HAT OFF HIS HEAD AND TAKING HIS SHILLELAGH OFF HIM
Stop it. You're meant to look like a Catholic not bloody Darby O'Gill

UNCLE ANDY:
Right have I got this right. It's not Ulster, it's the occupied six counties.

DYMPNA:
Or

UNCLE ANDY:
the orange statelet.

DYMPNA:
And a traditional route is?

UNCLE ANDY:
A sectarian coat trailing exercise.

BILLY:
GRABBING NOTES OFF HIM
And what are Sinn Fein?

UNCLE ANDY:
A legitimate political party with an electoral mandate

BILLY:
And they have?....

UNCLE ANDY:
DISGUSTED
No connection with the IRA. And they say taigs have no sense of humour. Right come on lets go.

HE WALKS TO THE DOOR WITH HIS FAMOUS UNCLE ANDY WALK

DYMPNA:
No, no, no what are you doing?

UNCLE ANDY:
Wha?

DYMPNA:
You're walking like a Protestant. You might as well put a bowler hat and sash on. Try and walk like a Catholic.

UNCLE ANDY:
What way?

DYMPNA: Well a bit more..

SHE SLOUCHES AND ADOPTS A SLACK GAIT AND STARES DOWN AT THE GROUND. SHE EXITS THROUGH THE FRONT DOOR. UNCLE ANDY AND BILLY LOOK AT EACH OTHER ADOPT SAME STANCE AND SHUFFLE OUT THE FRONT DOOR

SCENE EP 3/11. CHURCH. EXT. (DAY 6). DAY LIGHT. MORNING.

DA, MA IN THE USUAL WEDDING GEAR AND SEAMUS RYAN ARE AT THE DOOR OF THE CHURCH. SEAMUS IS STILL WEARING A LEATHER JACKET AND JEANS, HE IS SPORTING A CARNATION IN HONOUR OF THE DAY. UNCLE ANDY, BILLY AND DYMPNA WALK UP STILL DOING THEIR "CATHOLIC" WALK

UNCLE ANDY:
Alright Da.

DA:
Alright Uncle An... Rory.

MA:
Hi you Billy.

DA:
Liam! Liam! He's Liam.

UNCLE ANDY, BILLY, AND DYMPNA HEAD ON THROUGH

GROAN!

MA:
Aye he is walking funny.

WE SEE THE BACK OF TWO PEOPLES HEADS: GERRY ADAMS AND MARTIN MCGUINNESS AS THEY HEAD INTO THE CHURCH PAST THE PARENTS

DA:
NODDING A GREETING
Gerry... Martin.....I thought they were supposed to be in Washington today.

SEAMUS:
They wouldn't turn down an invite from me. Ah here's the boys.

A WHITE HIACE VAN SCREECHES TO A HALT AND A STREAM OF LEATHER JACKETED YOUNG MEN ALL

SPORTING CARNATIONS POUR OUT OF THE VAN IN UNFEASIBLY LARGE NUMBERS THEY PROCEED TO FILE PAST THE PARENTS INTO THE CHURCH

MA:
Is Mrs Ryan not coming today?

SEAMUS:
No she can't be with us she's in hospital having a baby.

MA:
Oh lovely do you know what it is?

SEAMUS:
I'm hoping for a boy.

CUT TO NEXT SCENE

SCENE EP 3/12. CHURCH. INT. STUDIO. (DAY 6). DAY LIGHT. MORNING.

CAL IS SITTING IN A PEW SURROUNDED BY THE BOYS SIMON IS SITTING NEXT TO HIM. HE LEANS INTO CAL

give my head peace

Damon looked better here than he did on his actual wedding day – but if you are going to insist on a traditional stag night!

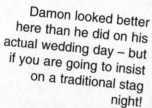

The wedding was stopped for a spot of staring.

SIMON:
We meant what we said you know.

THE CAMERA SWITCHES TO UNCLE ANDY, BILLY, DYMPNA, MA AND DA SITTING IN THE FRONT ROW

UNCLE ANDY:
What's the hymn sheet for.

DA:
Just wait and see.

THE ORGAN STARTS WITH AN INTRODUCTORY FUGUE UNTIL IT STARTS TO PLAY A SLOW VERSION OF "THE MEN BEHIND THE WIRE". THE CONGREGATION STAND AS SEAMUS AND THE VEILED BRIDE START TO WALK DOWN THE AISLE. SHE HAS A COMEDY PREGNANT BUMP.

THE CONGREGATION STANDS AND STARTS TO SING. UNCLE ANDY LOOKS ASKANCE BUT IS ELBOWED BY BILLY AND STARTS TO SING

ALL:
Armoured cars and tanks and guns
Came to take away our sons

And every man will stand behind the men behind the wire.

THE BRIDE AND SEAMUS HAVE ARRIVED AT THE ALTAR. A PRIEST IS ALSO STANDING THERE. CAL IS PUSHED TO THE FRONT BY THE BROTHERS. THE BRIDE LIFTS THE VEIL. IT IS THE SINGLE GIRL FROM THE DISCO

CAL:
You.

BRIDE:
Him! I'm not marrying him that's the "wow" man.

SEAMUS:
You'll marry who I'll say you'll marry.

CAL:
Well if the girl doesn't want to get married....

HE MAKES TO LEAVE BUT IS PENNED BACK BY THE BOYS

SIMON:
What seems to be the problem.

CAL:
It's her she doesn't want to go through with it.

SIMON:
MENACINGLY
You're not even married and you've upset our sister already.

SEAMUS:
TO THE PRIEST
Get on with it father.

CAL:
No! I'm not doing it, no! You can do whatever you want I'm not marrying her.

SEAMUS:
I think it would be better if Gerry and Martin left. I don't want them to see this.

MA:
You better get up there and do something.

DA:
Now Ma you should never interfere between a man and his wife.

MA:
They're not married yet. Get up there.

DA GETS UP RELUCTANTLY

DYMPNA:
Billy get up there and help my Da.

BILLY:
FEIGNING IGNORANCE
Lovely church this and the flowers are beaut.....

DYMPNA:
Get up there.

**BILLY GETS UP
RELUCTANTLY**

UNCLE ANDY:
GETTING UP
I'll go as well...I want a better view.

CUT BACK TO ALTAR

CAL:
TO THE RYAN'S
I'm not the father of that baby and I'm not doing it.

UNCLE ANDY:
You tell him son.

CAL:
You can't make me.

UNCLE ANDY:
That's right Cal you take no crap. What can they do there's only about thirty of them.

Cal finds that the church has been double-booked by a convention of clones.

Uncle Andy has discovered that the hymn sheet is in Irish. Ma covers up her ignorance of the 'mother tongue' by humming along.

DA:
You're really not helping here.

BRIDE:
POINTING AT UNCLE ANDY
You! What are you doing here.

UNCLE ANDY:
LOOKING ROUND HIMSELF
Sorry love.

SEAMUS:
Who's this?

BRIDE:
He's the one! He's the father of my child.

UNCLE ANDY:
A wha.

DA:
Him? He couldn't be the father.

SEAMUS:
What's his name, Rory O'...

DA:
Rory O nothing. He's Uncle Andy, a notorious Protestant, Orangeman and Loyalist

SEAMUS:
NODDING AT MA'S STATEMENT AND SHAKING WITH RAGE
Protestant, Orangeman and Loyalist.

MA:
I take it this means the weddings off?

BILLY:
A word of advice Uncle Andy: run like a catholic.

CUT HARD TO NEXT SCENE

SCENE EP 3/13. LANDROVER. EXT. (DAY 6). DAY LIGHT. AFTERNOON.

BILLY AND UNCLE ANDY AND DYMPNA ARE SITTING IN THE FRONT. BILLY HAS FOOT DOWN THEY ARE CLEARLY DISHEVELLED AND SWEATY FROM RUNNING TO ESCAPE THE BOYS

BILLY:
Any sign of that hiace van?

DYMPNA:
No I think we lost them at Sandy Row.

BILLY:
I am sick of you. Of all the things you've done that takes the biscuit.

UNCLE ANDY:
It wasn't me.

BILLY:
That's it. First thing on Monday morning I'm taking you to see a doctor.

DYMPNA:
It's not a doctor he needs Billy, it's a vet.

UNCLE ANDY:
Look I'm telling ye I never met the girl before in my life. It wasn't me.

BILLY:
Oh aye it was that double of yours again wasn't it. There's somebody looks like you, dresses like you, goes running round town impregnating woman and blaming you.

UNCLE ANDY:
There must be.

BILLY/ DYMPNA:
TOGETHER
Ballix!

WE SEE THE LANDROVER PASS DOWN A STREET IT DRIVES PAST A PEDESTRIAN WHO IS THE EXACT DOUBLE OF UNCLE ANDY HE LOOKS LIKE UNCLE ANDY, DRESSES LIKE UNCLE ANDY, WALKS LIKE UNCLE ANDY AND IS PLAYED BY MARTY REID

RUN TITLES

MARTY WANTS TO KNOW DOES THIS MEAN HE GETS TWO FEES ?